ONLY HUMAN

T
b.
dɑ

ONLY HUMAN
21ST CENTURY COP

GEMMA HINES

The Book Guild Ltd

First published in Great Britain in 2017 by
The Book Guild Ltd
9 Priory Business Park
Wistow Road, Kibworth
Leicestershire, LE8 0RX
Freephone: 0800 999 2982
www.bookguild.co.uk
Email: info@bookguild.co.uk
Twitter: @bookguild

Typeset in Minion Pro

Printed and bound in Great Britain by
CPI Group (UK) Ltd, Croydon, CR0 4YY

ISBN 978 1912083 510

British Library Cataloguing in Publication Data.
A catalogue record for this book is available from the British Library.

I would like to dedicate this book to my fallen friends
Ian Rowley
Nicola Hughes
Fiona Bone
Tracey Miskell
Andrew Summerscales

All real-life incidents that I have included in this book have had the names, dates and places changed to protect the identity of all those involved. This is of course apart from the above five colleagues whom I have dedicated this book to.

I would like to thank the amazing supportive people I have around me daily who have pulled me through the darkest of days and stood by my side no matter what,
my two beautiful children Grace and Harley,
my coach and best friend Chris,
And
My Dad.

You all know who you are and to you all I am eternally grateful.
FAMILY IS EVERYTHING
Much love
Gem x

IN THE BEGINNING

Before I joined the police, I was a fitness instructor, aerobics instructor and personal trainer. I had been on my work experience in Year 10 of school and had pretty much blagged my way into a full-time cleaning job at a well-known gym. When I left school, I was promoted to work in the gym as a leisure assistant and worked my way up the ranks. I had managed to work there from the age of fifteen to nineteen years and during this time, due to my age, training courses were offered to me for free in abundance. I was like a sponge; I attended everything I possibly could and gathered as much information as I could. I had completed a Level 2 and 3 NVQ in Sport and Leisure and then various YMCA courses such as: Nutrition and Weight Management, Exercise to Music, Gym Instructor and Lifeguard courses. I had pretty much completed as many courses that were on offer and had a choice. I was stuck in a rut due to never actually being challenged. The gym in which I worked was a hotel gym with a highly priced joining fee and a monthly fee meaning the clientele were well off. They were generally older and rich. Most of my clients were over 30 with weight problems. I didn't have anything that I could sink my teeth into, nothing that challenged me. I had to either branch out and become self-employed or look for a more challenging job.

At eighteen years old I was very independent and had lived a colourful life, being self-sufficient and living away from parents and family from the age of 15. At 18 I was still young and naive and doubted that I would have the maturity to run my own business successfully. I decided to start job hunting. Cheekily, I used the works gym computer to do my searching as I couldn't afford a computer of my own, let alone Wi-Fi or internet. Whilst deep in concentration searching the internet, a member peered over my shoulder, and seeing that I was job hunting he suggested I might consider the police force. At first I pretty much laughed in his face, I had next to no academic qualifications after leaving school and didn't think very highly of myself. I didn't think I was like any of the cops I had ever met. In my eyes, I placed them on a pedestal; coming from unbroken homes, people don't make mistakes and that certainly didn't describe me. The cops I had met were all much older than me, very stern and pretty scary. The member suggested that it may be a good idea to apply for the Special Constables, and with nothing to lose that's exactly what I did.

I was totally gobsmacked when I passed the application process and was invited down to Sedgley Park for an interview. I attended, having never had an interview in my entire life before and was knocked off my feet when they offered me the job. My thoughts were, "Why on earth would they want me?"

So, in 2003 I became a Special Constable. I met some new recruits and picked up my brand spanking new uniform. We completed our attestation where we all swore an oath and were given our policing powers and warrant cards. We then attended three or four weekends where we were taught the basics of law. Then we attended a small amount of self-defence training where we were taught how to defend ourselves, how to use our baton, handcuffs and CS spray. After a scarily short amount of time, I was allowed out on the streets with a tutor to fight crime and protect people.

What they don't explain to you in training is that your uniform is exactly the same as any full-time police officer and you have the exact same powers. The only thing that can differentiate you between a full-time officer and a special constable is the collar number on your epaulettes on your shoulder. However, when a member of the public approaches, they haven't a clue about any of that; they see your uniform and expect you to solve all their life problems. When the shit hits the fan, it doesn't matter if you are out on your first shift or have been in the job for years; the public expect you to help them and God help you if you can't.

In the beginning, I was always with another officer. I preferred to go out on duty with the full-time response officers who we called the "REGS" (regular full-time officers). I liked these shifts better as these officers were always sent to the most urgent jobs and often got stuck into the jobs that required you to attend with your blue lights and sirens on. I remember being on my first blue light run in a police car as a Special Constable. I held onto the handrail and the adrenaline was pumping through my veins; we were travelling really fast, going through red lights, overtaking vehicles with the blue lights on and the sirens sounding. Whilst doing all this I was expected to find our destination in the paper A-Z as cop cars are not fitted with sat navs. It was a massive adrenaline rush. I loved every second and knew I wanted to do much more of this type of job.

Most regular officers were happy to have another officer to pair up with for the shift, it allowed them to have the added backup and someone to talk to. However, I did find that many old-school officers despised Special Constables. To them, if Special Constables didn't exist they may be paid more and they would be given more overtime. Whilst Specials were around, many officers found them to be incompetent and lazy. This may have been the case for some; however, for most Special Constables incompetence came from a lack of knowledge and a lack of the REGS' willingness to pass on their knowledge.

I remember working with a REG one night who didn't quite mind Specials. We were given a job on a Grade 1 urgent marker and he passed me his A-Z and told me to find the address and direct him in. I must have been looking for too long as he pulled over and snatched it off me and found the address himself in literally less than 30 seconds. He explained to me afterwards that all the road names were listed in the back of the book and that then directs you to the correct page and grid reference of the street. I honestly felt so stupid; I had never had any reason to ever use an A-Z before so would never have known this without being shown. Another time I felt daft was when I was asked to spell a person's name over the radio phonetically; "SUGAR, MIKE, INDIA, TRAIN, HOTEL". The problem with the police radio is that everybody on a whole division can hear you, so once again I was the joke of the evening.

As a Special Constable, I remember my first arrest well. I arrested a young lad for Section 16a of the Firearms Act. He had basically been with his mate in his mate's banger of a car and they had been driving around the area all evening, firing a paintball gun out of the car window at people and petrol forecourt signs. We had originally spent about an hour looking around for the car in question but called off the search after we failed to locate it. Approximately 3 hours later in a completely different area, I spotted the car. When we pulled up alongside the car I found a guy in the driver's seat, a guy in the passenger seat with a paintball gun on his lap and a massive bag of unused paintballs in the centre console. They were caught red-handed. I was so nervous and I told the guy holding the gun that he was under arrest and put him in the back of the police van but forgot to caution him. When we arrived at the custody office I remembered the police caution and in a tongue-tied manner read it aloud to him. Whilst doing so, I placed the paintball gun and the pellets on the custody desk.

This man mountain of a Sergeant stood up over me and began bellowing a barrage of abuse at me; he was really angry and was going completely red in the face. As he shouted at me he was spitting in my face. It was on this day that I learned the hard way that I should never, ever take any type of gun into a custody office, not even a paintball gun. I remember excusing myself before running to the ladies and bawling my eyes out.

I soon met a varied number of cops, some young, some old, some wise, some arrogant. I made sure I did as many shifts as I could and whilst working at the gym five days a week, I made sure I worked every Friday, Saturday and Sunday night. It was at this time I managed to get a pretty good picture of what policing was really like. At the end of 2005, I took a leap of faith and applied to the full-time police.

I passed the paper sift and the assessment centre, the medical and the fitness test and then went to Sedgley Park for my final interview. For someone who never actually wanted to be a cop, I was now extremely hopeful and excited about the possibility of this new adventure. I had never been in a formal interview in my life and didn't know what to expect at all. During the interview, I panicked and at the end when they told me that I had failed I actually cried. I went away thinking that I had to wait 6 months to reapply and start all over again which is the normal procedure. I was devastated. I went back to the gym and continued to look for more jobs. Two weeks later I received a phone call asking me back for a second interview. I was confused but excited. Whilst on duty as a Special, I approached one of the Chief Inspectors and asked for advice on interviews. He really helped and I went back and smashed the second interview and bagged myself the job as a full-time police officer. I was now twenty years old and was going to be a real-life police officer!

In March 2006, I was attested and swore the oath to protect and serve with honesty and integrity. It was a really proud day for me and I felt like I had come some way in overcoming my life struggles and had finally made it.

I didn't really know what to expect. The training system had changed drastically within the police. Budgets had been cut massively, meaning the old residential training school Bruche had closed. We were told early on that most of our training would be completed at Sedgley Park in Prestwich. We were also told that a lot of our training would be completed out in the community. We were informed that this was to enable better community cohesion, bridging the gap between the public and the police.

It turns out that this was a big cover up; the trainers and senior leadership team within GMP were not interested in community cohesion at all. The placements were free, costing not one penny to the police force, saving them a fortune. I guess they sold it to the local authority that whilst police officers were being trained in their venues, they would be safe and free from crime.

We trained at a primary school during the summer holidays, completely out of sight of the community. At other times, we trained in a local shopping centre in a back room of the staff area completely out of sight of the general public. Many of the trainers came from Bruche and had been teaching police officers for a good number of years. You had different types of trainers and this list is not complete:

1. The intelligent trainer who was good at their job, explained things properly on all levels and had a good knowledge of what they were teaching. If you had a question they would never make you feel daft for asking it and would generally know the answer and if they did not, they would find it out for you. I came across only one trainer in my entire policing career that fitted this description.

2. The nearly retired guy who went into training as an easy option, to see out their remaining service prior to leaving the job. This is the guy who thought that they knew it all, but actually didn't have a clue when asked questions that were not listed on the paper in front of their faces. They generally

dealt with people asking these questions by ridiculing them in front of the class to ensure they didn't ask any questions again.

3. The officer on the Excellerate programme through GMP who must do a spell in the training department before they are promoted. Academically, these guys are generally quite clever but for what they have in brains they lack in common sense and people skills.

4. A member of the sick, lame and lazy, or an officer who wants to work a Monday to Friday 9–5 job. When people are on long term sick in the police and return on restricted duties, they are placed in a role that takes them away from front-line duties. They are then placed in a role that requires no confrontation or contact with the public. When people have a genuine illness then this suits them quite well and they seem to thrive in the training environment; however, when people fake an illness or problem, they go to training to hide and not get noticed for their lazy ways. These trainers don't really have a clue about what they are teaching due to never actually spending more than 5 minutes on front-line duties.

5. Finally, the trainer who has been in the job for that long that they can wing their way through the training by constantly telling war stories of "back in the day" with a bit of law knowledge thrown in for good effect.

I struggled academically throughout my police training with the paper tests we were given. The new learning format was called a SOLAP. This stood for Student Officer Learning and Assessment Portfolio. It was basically the same format as an NVQ. I had already completed two of those back at the gym, so I should have really sailed through the course. I did not however, as every morning we would arrive at the venue for 7am, and spend the next hour waiting for a trainer to actually show up. When they eventually showed, they would piss around for the next half an hour and then place the learning material for the day on the overhead projector for us to read. Funnily enough, each time this was done it appeared to be the very first time that the trainer had read it also. Planning and preparation for our classes seemed to be far beyond their capabilities.

THE EARLY DAYS

In the past 10 years, I have experienced ups and downs both in my personal life and on the job. I have learned many lessons and have witnessed many incidents that have changed my outlook on life and my opinion on people in general. You would assume that in a professional organisation such as the Police Force that their officers would act in accordance with the law and be professional always, both in work and out of work. This, unfortunately, is not always the case and I have had my eyes opened to the dark side of policing.

I experienced bullying from the very start of my policing career. They employed eighty new students in our intake divided into four classes of twenty. Each class was made up from a variety of people from all ages, and all social backgrounds. Most of the younger guys clicked straight away and began socialising out of work. I wasn't a big drinker and had just bought a derelict house so spent my free time mainly turning it into a home. I was the odd one out, along with a young Asian lad, as we couldn't make many of the planned nights out boozing on the town. The Asian lad, Saj, was a really nice guy who chose to spend time at home with his family instead of going out drinking. After a few weeks, once everybody had settled into the group and small cliques were formed, the bullying began. Small little bits at first, taking the piss out of his accent. If Saj gave an incorrect answer within a group discussion they would jeer or nudge one another, whispering loudly enough for Saj to hear their taunts. When we had to get ourselves into groups for class discussions, the others would turn their backs on him and completely exclude him. I sat and watched this behaviour for a while, certain that I wasn't the only one that should be noticing it. I was new to the job and had never dealt with anything like this before but I was quite sure that the class trainers should be picking up on this kind of behaviour. I sat back and watched the trainers brush each insult, each jeer off as harmless banter, but could clearly see that Saj was becoming increasingly distant and his enjoyment of the course was waning. In the end, I couldn't take any more of it so after the class one day, I had a quiet word with one of the trainers. I explained to him that not only was I disgusted that Saj was being bullied in such a way, but more disgusted that no trainer had yet dealt with this situation.

I assumed that the main ringleaders were spoken to on the side and told of my complaint as a few of them stopped speaking to me, but thankfully the bullying stopped for Saj. Luckily, it didn't stop Saj from progressing in his career and he is still a police officer being promoted within the ranks.

During the initial training course, the trainers continued to make poor decisions and were not the squeaky clean, politically correct officers I would expect as the people training front-line officers. In a class of twenty officers there were three females including myself, all adults, all learning at different levels. The male instructors, at one point during the course, made a rule that female officers were not allowed to sit together. Why I do not know but I just assumed that it was another power trip. On my final one to one discussion with the trainer who had pulled my name out of the hat, prior to going back to the division as a fully trained officer, a confusing conversation took place. The officer was called Martin and he was almost retired; he had spent most of his years in the traffic department and was one of the worst trainers we had been landed with, as he didn't have a clue about 21st century criminal law. I am the first to admit that

I do not learn in an academic environment and generally do not do well in academic tests; however, when learning through role play and on the job, I have been known to excel. This trainer Martin highlighted these facts to me during the final one to one and his parting words, "You won't have any problems in the cops, you'll get by on your looks alone, brains aren't everything."

I wanted to slap him in his face! Cheeky git. I wanted to do well in my job because I was good at it, not because certain officers may think that my looks would take me far.

I have had the discussion about "POSITIVE DISCRIMINATION" a hundred times over. I have argued until I am blue in my face and it has never ever got me anywhere. I believe that in any job, the people who prove that they can do it the best should be given the opportunities. I certainly do not believe that you should be able to sail through the ranks on basis of gender, skin colour, sexual orientation, religion or disability. I have been told far too many times that certain groups of people are underrepresented within the police, but in my opinion this is crap. Why should you be discriminated against and not given opportunities based on gender, skin colour, sexual orientation, religion or disability and flipping that on its head, why should these things alone allow you more opportunity? I believe that skills and talent should get you further in your job, along with hard work and determination to make a difference. Maybe knowing an extra language or being good with people, not based on the other categories previously mentioned. On the back of this, the way the police force hire their staff now has drastically changed. Many officers such as myself wouldn't have a chance of getting in the job if we were to reapply today. Now you must have attended college and university to apply, this breeds a force of academics and people lacking in people skills and common sense. The officer who truly represents the areas in which we work is a dying breed and soon the police force as we know it will be dead and buried.

POLICE MISUSE OF POWER
INTERNALLY AND EXTERNALLY

Bullying didn't just happen colleague to colleague. Some officers joined the job with the intention of helping others and making a difference. Other officers put on their uniform and used it like a tool of power. They became arrogant, and rude, and believed that the law didn't apply to them. Throughout the past 10 years, I have seen many officers on a power trip misusing their powers. The way I dealt with such things changed over the years as I became more confident and less accepting of such behaviour. I could list endless times when I have had to witness and challenge officers' bad behaviour; however, I have picked out the incidents that have remained with me throughout the years.

When I was early in my probation, I was tasked with standing at various points of a local hotel situated in a poverty and crime stricken housing estate, guarding a murder scene. I spent three days on that murder scene, guarding varying points throughout my duties. Whilst I was there, many of the young people from the estate came for a nosey. They were trying to find out details of the incident in their own cheeky ways; they understood a murder had been committed as news travelled faster than the cops on the estate. Like any council estate people are close and with the age of mobile technology not many secrets are kept. I know this only too well as this is the kind of estate I had spent my childhood on. During the time I was there, these young people, who were mainly lads, caused me no trouble at all. They were polite and respectful in their own cheeky way. A couple of them were sporting their electronically monitored tags around their legs, giving a clear indication that they were well known for their own personal criminal convictions. However, at no point would this have ever changed the way I spoke with these lads; to me they were polite and respectful so why would I treat them in any other manner than with respect? There were several officers dotted around the scene and when it neared the end of my shift the handover shift arrived. A cop who was of the old-school type came to my location. I didn't know him to talk to as I didn't like him; he was almost up for retirement and was one of the most arrogant men I had ever come across. He stood over 6ft tall, a large heavy build; I felt him approach before I had even seen him. I had my back to him and was explaining to one of the local young lads that it was time for my shift to end so he should go and get some tea. The officer, completely blanking me, walked straight up to the young lad, grabbed him around his throat with his shovel like hands and pushed him hard up against the wall. He shouted in his face.

"I thought I told you to fuck off and not come back."

The young lad only seconds before was sweet and respectful, now he was full of expletives and telling the officer to get the fuck off him as he had done nothing wrong. Before I could do or say anything, the officer dropped the lad and he ran off. I was petrified of this officer myself let alone this lad he had just had by his throat. Despite my fear I still asked him why he did what he did; his reply was plain and simple without any remorse,

"These little shits need to know who's boss."

I was mortified. This cop was a bully and I wanted nothing more to do with him. On the way back to the station, I explained to another cop, who was a fair few years older than me with a lot more life experience, what I had seen. I was told not to ever mention it again as the offending officer would just deny it. I didn't know the kid's name, and the officer always did things like that and always gets away with it as he is well respected among supervision. He said nobody would believe a new probationer anyway. I hated what I had just witnessed, I hated that I felt helpless, it was at this point that I understood why some people hated the police.

There were various other incidents throughout the next few years, but as I gained confidence within my role, I learned exactly how to challenge what I believed was inappropriate behaviour.

In recent years, we were called to a young lad that was being restrained by his friends in a first floor flat. The caller to the police was frantic and described this young lad as being possessed. When you hear something like that on your way, you think it's a little farfetched and over exaggerated but when I arrived, I witnessed my first case of Acute Behavioural Disorder or Excited Delirium as it's also known. I had only ever heard of this in training sessions and in short video clips within the training.

In front of me I found a lad who looked eight stone wet through, with the most aggressive, super human strength I have ever witnessed of a person his size. He was being pinned down by two grown men and when asked what he had taken they all shut up. The flat was small and in the living room there was the lad being pinned down by two of his mates, myself and another two cops. The floor length window was open and the male on the floor was trying to get over to it to get out. For his own safety, I stepped in with the other officers and we restrained him properly. There was an officer at his head, an officer by his side and an officer on his legs. I placed him in handcuffs to the front so that he couldn't hit out and remained by his legs.

There were now three officers present and not one of us had any personal issue leg restraints. In my opinion, if we could restrain his legs and then take our hands off him, this lad had a better chance of getting through this ordeal uninjured. I requested leg restraints over the radio and finally another two officers arrived. I placed these around his legs and then told all the officers to get off the guy. All but one took their hands off him. The one officer who was by his head was pushing it hard into the floor. I told him to get off but still he refused. I have good knowledge of the human body due to doing anatomy and physiology during my time as a personal trainer and knew that with ABD the likelihood of this guy's heart stopping was extremely high. I was not having him die on me so again told the officer to back off. He looked at me and told me that it was his own fault for being a dick and taking drugs.

I looked at the male and it became clear that despite his extreme violence and super strength he wasn't directing it at anyone but himself. It looked like he was having a battle with something deep inside of him. He kept saying, "GET IT OUT OF ME, HELP ME!" and was thrashing around on the floor, biting his own tongue and the inside of his mouth. He was trying to harm himself, not the officers so again I told the officer to back off. Eventually he did and even the Sergeant saw what was happening but said nothing.

Whilst we were waiting for the paramedics, I took the sofa cushions off the couch and placed them around him to prevent him from banging against the TV cabinet. When they did finally arrive, they stated that there was nothing they could do where he was and asked if we could carry him down to the ambulance, as he was still up on the first floor. It took five officers to carefully carry him down the stairs and place him on the stretcher which the paramedics strapped him to. They couldn't conduct any checks on him in the ambulance due to his violence so turned on their blue lights and sirens and got him to the hospital as quickly as they could. The officer who had used excessive force was in the rear of the ambulance with me and the paramedic. Every time we went over a bump, he purposely fell on the man and hit him or nudged him to wind him up. I told him to stop and reminded him that there was CCTV in ambulances. I just thought he was a total dick to be honest.

When we arrived at the hospital, the male was placed in the Resus and when he was linked up to the ECG heart monitor, it showed that his resting heart rate was 180bpm. That is when he was strapped to a bed and not moving; whilst we were restraining him in his flat, I'm assuming he was seconds from a major heart attack, given what I had just been told. I realised how important it was to make the decision to take our hands off him once he was in leg restraints. The fact that no officer at the scene had any personal issue restraints sickened me and could have made the difference between life and death. When I returned to the police station, I made it my business to ensure every officer on my shift had a pair of personal issue restraints. It transpired that the male had smoked a legal (illegal) high called Spice, along with taking cocaine. This had caused his severe behaviour. This is another job I wish I'd been allowed to film, to show youngsters exactly why they shouldn't touch any drugs.

The same officer in the previous incident has misused his powers many times before. He would go into houses in which we needed to search for offenders; he would leave the house in a total mess on purpose and pour bubble bath down the toilet, or find all the porn and sex toys in the house and line them up on the bedroom shelf, knowing full well that no one would ever ring in to complain through their embarrassment. Many times, he has given prisoners an extra dig and is well known in the custody office for winding compliant prisoners up before arriving. Supervision were aware of his behaviour but it was never raised or challenged. The same officer completed his Sergeant's exam and spent time as an acting Sergeant This is the crap thing about the police; officers of this type are eligible to climb the ranks and become supervisors, meaning the trust from the public is waning.

Many old, male, old-school officers are still of the opinion that women shouldn't be doing the job as a front-line officer. Many of them feel that women don't have the strength to restrain somebody if so required and I heard many officers say that they would rather have a bloke back them up than a woman. I've also heard many sexist comments aimed in my direction, "Women should be in the kitchen", "women in the police are only useful for one thing and that's looking after the children". There have been a few occasions when a male supervisor has given a female PC a certain job, just because of her gender and I don't think that in this day and age this should be happening. People should be assigned to specific roles based on their competencies, not based on whether a bloke thinks it's a woman's job or not.

I believe that if a man and a woman can both pass the same physical tests for the role then they should be treated equally. If a role required a person to lift a certain amount of weight, then I believe that male or female, they should be made to prove they can do it first by way of a test. For example, whilst I was a police officer, I was trained to use the police wham ram. Also known as The Enforcer, this is an object that is made of steel, with a steel pad at the end so it can absorb the impact. It has a handle at the opposite end so that an officer can swing it accurately, without using their own added strength. The Enforcer can apply more than three tonnes of impact force to door locks. It is only 58cm and weighs in at 16kg. Due to it being so heavy, many female officers struggled to complete the course as they couldn't lift The Enforcer let alone swing it. I, at no point, thought that anything was wrong with certain officers, both male and female, being turned away from the course if they couldn't lift The Enforcer. I also think that if the role requires a certain level of strength and fitness that should not be lowered based on the person's gender.

I remember when the annual fitness test came in for all

police officers. This consists of running an old-school 'bleep test'. It requires an officer to run between two points, 15 metres apart, to a series of bleeps. The level that you must reach is level 5.4 and this is barely breaking into a jog. In my opinion, it falls way below the requirement of a front-line officer and if you cannot pass the test, then you should not be a police officer on the front line. Many officers have failed this yearly test and so far, I haven't heard of one being taken off front-line duties as a result. There are too many unfit overweight officers in the force these days.

I have experienced sexism many times, one time in particular made me chuckle when the result happened. A couple of officers attended a report of a robbery at a local Holland and Barrett where £300 in cash was taken by a very distinctive Asian male. From the description, two of my colleagues attended a local address to check for an offender who matched it. On their arrival, the door was ajar and the bloke was making his way into the loft. As one of my colleagues went to grab him, he swung a large machete type knife through the loft hatch towards his head. The hatch then closed.

Many officers were called to the address, including myself, the Sergeant and the Acting Inspector. This is the same Inspector that I will allude to later in my book, in the suicide section. Once inside, the Inspector decided to contact a Force Negotiator and the Tactical Aid Unit. I went back to the police station to pick up mine and a few other officers' NATO helmets and public order protective clothing, along with shields. We are all trained to the same level and have proved ourselves through training that we are all equal, male and female. Despite this, the Inspector questioned why I had brought my own kit and said he only wanted the men kitting up. He told me to go and stand at the front door so no one else could enter the house. I was fuming with him but didn't argue as there were more pressing issues to be dealing with. Whilst at the front I let the negotiator in who started to engage and talk to the man in the loft. There were also two female officers around the back of the address, keeping an eye on it from that angle.

It had been going on for a good hour and I could still hear the negotiator talking inside when I heard one of the neighbours on the terraced street shout me over. There, next to him, was the man that fitted the description of the robber. He was limping, covered in insulation and filthy. I ran over and took hold of him, placing him in cuffs. I told him that he was under arrest for robbery. He was all sweaty and the neighbours said they had just seen him climb down their drain pipe and fall on the floor.

I radioed through to the Inspector who was still in the house. I asked if the negotiator was still talking to the male offender and I was told that they hadn't heard anything for a while but he was still trying to engage him. I explained to them that the reason he was quiet was because he was outside with me under arrest in handcuffs. I heard tumbleweed on the radio and heard heavy footsteps coming down the stairs of the house and outside. The front door opened and out came the male Inspector, a full Tactical Aid Unit of big burly men, all in full PSU gear with NATO helmets on, the other three male officers dressed in their full PSU gear and NATO helmets, followed by the negotiator. There I stood, a mere female 5ft 4 in height, normal day uniform, holding the suspect around his arm whilst he was in handcuffs.

I didn't have to say anything to the Inspector, my face said it all. I think by merely dealing with the situation before telling him, I had proved my point.

It turned out that the guy who I arrested had been walking back and forth whilst talking to the negotiator, removing the bricks that separated the two houses' lofts. He then removed some of the roof tiles and climbed out onto it, attempted to shimmy down the drain pipe and fell when he was half way down. When he was taken to the custody office, he was strip searched as he had a history of concealing things in inappropriate places.

When this was conducted, the £300 that had been stolen from Holland and Barrett was in a rolled-up wad shoved right up his backside. He was made to pull it out himself and it was placed in a money bag. I was thankful to be a woman at that point as I didn't have to conduct the strip search or count the cash that would, undoubtedly, smell terrible.

I'M ONLY HUMAN

As a young female, I found myself becoming increasingly broody and desperate to start my own family. I felt that I had a stable career and was in a stable relationship, living with my partner of 2 years who was also a police officer. We decided to try for a child and in February 2009 I got the news that I was pregnant with our little girl. She was due in October 2009. During my pregnancy, I was removed from front-line duties and placed in an admin role, away from the general public. My role consisted of event planning, issuing Inspectors and Supervisors with cancelled rest days to allow other Inspectors and Supervisors to take annual leave. It was a very stressful role that I found harder than the actual role of a front-line officer. I wasn't made for sitting behind a desk, I was born to help people on the front line. I was often berated by disgruntled Inspectors in front of an open office full of staff for giving them too many cover days, spoken to like a piece of dirt despite the ever-growing baby in my belly. My pregnancy didn't go swimmingly and at 13 weeks pregnant I was rushed into hospital and told that I had potentially lost my baby. After a gruelling 12-hour wait, I received an ultrasound and heard my daughter's heartbeat. It was probably the single most amazing sound I have ever heard, at a time when I expected to hear nothing. The next few months went well; I was constantly monitored, as was my child. I had planned to work right up until my due date if I possibly could and that would allow me more time off with our baby when she arrived. My relationship with my partner was very unstable. I had sold my house to move in with him; I had moved with nothing other than the clothes that were in my wardrobe. I now lived in his house with his rules and I was not allowed to do anything without asking permission first. I paid half towards any decorations and home improvements but it was always referred to as his house not ours. As I was still working full time, I was contributing half towards the bills and shopping. If we ever had an argument, he told me to leave and get out of his house. I had disclosed to him many things about my childhood and upbringing and during arguments he would tell me that I was hated by my family and unloved by many others. He told me that I was weird and unstable. At this point I could have agreed with him; I was completely unstable. I was a hormonal pregnant woman of 23 years, trying to hold down a full-time job whilst not knowing if I was going to come home to somewhere to live or not. It was exhausting. I was made to feel, in my pregnant state, I was repulsive and unfit for anyone.

I became ill at the end of my pregnancy with bad migraines and serious swelling of my legs, hands and feet. It was about 6am and I was due to be in work at 7am when my waters broke. In a panic, I realised that my baby was coming 6 weeks prematurely and there was nothing I could do about it. After 17 and ½ hours of labour, an epidural and gas and air, my baby girl was born with the assistance of forceps. The forceps dinted and cut a line in her forehead and she looked like my mini Harry Potter.

Once she was born, I had an overwhelming urge to protect her and make sure nobody ever hurt her. I knew my partner was resentful that he had to leave the hospital and go home and couldn't stay with his daughter. I tried desperately to feed her myself and due to the size of her tiny head and my massive GG milk filled boobs, I was fighting a losing battle. I remember a really rude nurse coming into my side room at about 3am on the first night, she grabbed my boob and shoved it into my daughter's mouth with such force that she left a big bruise on me. My partner came back the following day with a bunch of the most beautiful flowers, new pyjamas and a few snacks as the hospital food was disgusting. As time went on I continued to struggle in feeding my baby naturally, she became floppy and lethargic and started to completely refuse to feed. I was told I could go home but was certain that something was wrong with my baby. I was a first-time mum and nobody would take me seriously; even my partner was telling me to get our daughter ready so we could leave and it was clear I was starting to embarrass him and get on his nerves. I knew something was wrong so I refused to move until my daughter was fully examined by a paediatric doctor. The examination was carried out and the doctor seemed concerned. He ordered an urgent blood test and when the results returned our room filled with medical people. They took my baby out of my arms and wrapped her in a blanket, placing her in an old pram that belonged to the ward we were on. They rushed her out of the room and told me and my partner to follow. On the way, they explained that she had severe jaundice, she was extremely dehydrated and her bilirubin levels were just below the requirement for a full blood transfusion. The neonatal unit at Stepping Hill Hospital was closed for a refurbishment so she was taken on to the Treehouse ward and placed in a side room. She weighed 5lb 12 at birth and now due to lack of food and liquid she had lost weight. Her tiny arms with her tiny veins were too small to get a cannula in. It took four doctors to pin her down on a bed and try and get the line into her vein. She was screaming and I was a mess; I didn't want to leave her, I wanted to protect her but I felt helpless. Eventually they got the cannula in and she was placed on a drip of saline and sugar. Her eyes were covered with a bandage which looked like a pair of sunglasses, and she was laying in her cot under ultraviolet lights.

Over the next hour, myself and my partner sat staring at her little chest going up and down; luckily my best friend was a neo natal nurse at a local hospital so she explained exactly what was going on to me. The nurses on the ward barely came in at all due to being understaffed and busy. After a short while, the machine which she was linked up to started to bleep. She began to shake intermittently. I went to grab a nurse and when I eventually found one, she came in and said it was totally normal. She said that due to her being so used to being swaddled and now being naked under the lights, she must be feeling vulnerable. I believed her as she was the professional and I was a first-time mum. Over the next hour, the machine that she was linked up to bleeped many times and she looked like she was fitting whilst she was shaking. I asked various passing nurses to assist but each one gave the same answer that everything was fine. That was until 2 hours later, I finally had had enough and demanded a young nurse come and check my baby. She walked into the room and took one look at our daughter and then at the drip machine that she was linked up to and disconnected it, offering no explanation other than she had to go and speak to a supervisor. Approximately 5 minutes later, the highest ranking paediatric consultant that was on duty arrived in our room to explain that when our daughter was linked up to the drip machine they had made a mistake. Due to the neo natal unit being under renovation the nurses had placed our tiny baby on a toddler's drip and had pumped her tiny body with 11 ½ hours' worth of the saline and sugar over the past 2 hours. This is exactly why she was violently shaking and why the machine was bleeping. I was so angry, I wanted to wrap my tiny baby in her blanket and run her straight out of that hospital and protect her from everyone. I knew realistically that I couldn't do this as she still needed medical care but now I trusted no one with my baby girl.

When we left the hospital a week later, I had established feeding and despite continuously struggling to do so, I tried my best. I arrived home to a list of all the items my partner had bought whilst I was in hospital with our baby, written out clearly on the dining room table. He told me he had itemised the purchases so I could pay my half. The list included the expensive bunch of flowers he had bought for me, my pyjamas he had bought as I had to stay longer with our daughter and a shop he had done whilst I was in hospital, caring for our daughter. I was tired and didn't have the energy to argue so just agreed to pay my half. Family and friends descended on our house to meet our new arrival and all I wanted to do was lock the door and keep everyone away from her. When they came and held her, I took her back after a matter of minutes. In my head, if the medical professionals can mess up then anyone can and it was my job to protect her. My partner noticed that I was acting strange and offered to take her out to the shops to allow me some rest but I panicked and wouldn't let her out of my sight. I was petrified that if I wasn't with her I had no way of protecting her. She developed colic and was in pain every time I tried to feed her. My partner didn't help and began to tell me that I wasn't a good mum, that I wasn't doing the best for our daughter. The midwife attended, along with various health visitors who all told me and pushed me to continue breast feeding. Nobody gave me the advice to give my child a bottle, apart from my partner and he did it in such a way that he told me I was useless, a rubbish mum and that she needed a bottle so he could take over and feed her.

I went to a breast-feeding support group and tried my absolute best to do the best for my baby girl. Eventually, after 4 months, I decided to try her on a bottle. When I did she began to thrive, she started to put on weight, stopped suffering with colic and became a happy baby. This was not the same for me. I had developed major postnatal depression. I had major issues with leaving my baby, I wouldn't allow any family members to look after her. Her dad wasn't allowed to take her out without me being present as I was petrified that I wouldn't be able to protect her if I wasn't there. Her dad told me I was mental, that I was an unfit mother and that he was going to tell social services that I was crazy and I shouldn't be anywhere near our child. I was so scared that my daughter was going to be taken away from me, that when we moved her into her own room, I spent many nights on the floor sleeping next to her cot.

My partner began to isolate me from the outside world, I had dropped onto statutory maternity pay which totalled approximately £450 a month. I was now unable to pay half towards the bills and shopping as I once had and thus the daily insults began. I was called a tramp, a scroat, and a scrounger and told that I was a born and bred council estate girl, so should go back where I belonged. I had a car but struggled to pay for petrol as well as insurance and tax, my family and friends were 25 miles away and I couldn't afford to go and see them. I had a mobile phone on a contract, and used this to speak to family and friends but was made to feel guilty about the contract amount as he told me that I should have been contributing this money towards the bills. When my family came to see us, they were made to feel uncomfortable by my partner as he looked down on them for living in a council house. It didn't help with my anxiety around my daughter and eventually everybody I loved and cared about was pushed away. I was all alone and felt broken, he had convinced me that I was an unfit mother and I was petrified of every knock on the door, thinking that it would be social services coming to take my baby, or the mental health people coming to take me.

I was desperate and my partner told me that I would have to leave his house unless I went to the doctors for my mental health. He refused to come with me, so I sat in the waiting room scared and alone. I didn't know what I was going to say; when I was called in, I explained my fear at leaving my daughter and explained how low I was feeling. The female doctor simply looked at me and told me everything I was feeling was normal and that I should do some exercise, maybe go for a walk or something. When I returned home, my partner asked what medication I had been given, I told him that I hadn't been given anything and he went mad. He told me that he thought I was making it all up and laboured the fact that even a doctor didn't believe me. He said that I needed to change my ways or he would make me leave his house and leave our daughter with him. I was broken.

I considered taking my own life. I drove my car up to the moors and sat there for hours on end, considering driving off the cliff edge, thinking about what I couldn't offer my child compared to what her father could. Every single time I crumbled and couldn't bear the thought of her growing up without a mummy in her life so every night I drove home slowly, not wanting to arrive there again.

I remember as our child got older, she would mess up around the house as babies do, but due to his Obsessive-Compulsive Disorder he would return home from work and spend hours cleaning and telling me how much of a shite mother and partner I was. There were days that I sacrificed playing with my baby girl so that I could tidy the house and try and please her daddy when he got home. I'd make him tea and have her in bed sleeping soundly but he would come through the door and despite my efforts, point out what I had not done to his standard, even down to going through the cutlery drawer to locate any soap suds marks I had left on the knives. I was never, ever going to be good enough for him and in his head, I was never, ever going to be a good enough mother to our child.

I tried everything, I tried wearing my old smart clothes that were simply vest tops and jeans but I was told that the vest tops were too low cut and I shouldn't be wearing them as I was a mother now. I tried to do my makeup nicely, but was told that I wasn't very good at it and that I should go and ask various girls from work (I was given an actual list) for tips on how to do it. I was made to feel like I was worthless and I didn't realise what was happening at the time. I began to think it normal, not to want to go home, normal to drive around for hours on end to avoid the ultimatum of arriving home yet again.

Finally, the time arrived for me to return to work, our daughter was just over 1 year old and I still had the same petrified feelings about leaving her. About not being able to protect her. With a complete lack of empathy and care for me, my partner began telling me that if I didn't go back to work, then he would again kick me out of the house. He told me daily that I was a scroat and a scrounger living in his house without contributing. I tried explaining that £400 a month maternity pay only stretched so far for baby milk, clothes, fuel, and car tax and insurance. I was told that I should get my priorities right and put my child first, rather than worrying about fuel to get to friends and family. I was a completely broken woman.

When I eventually went back to work, I was placed on a Neighbourhood team, in a new area with a new team. I had no self-confidence left. Due to my partner being a police officer and believing that his role was more important than mine, I had to request a flexible working pattern that fitted in and around him. This meant that I would be working less hours and earning less money than him and at no point did he volunteer to assist me by altering his shifts. The flexible working plan I was on made it difficult for me to fit into any one team; however, I spent every day counting down the hours until I could get home and hold my daughter again.

My partner and I remained together simply because I felt I had nowhere else to go. I had very few friends and had pushed my family away so felt lonely. He continued to put me down daily, he would sit every night tap tapping away on his computer, speaking to anyone that wasn't me. If an argument began he would tell me to get out. I would go to work every day and struggle to deal with people's problems, knowing my life was in such a dire state. I hadn't the energy to climb out of the pit I had been shoved into. When my shifts ended, I'd make excuses to stay at work, around people that made me laugh and smile. When the Sergeant asked why I was still there, I told him that I couldn't face going home. When I had stayed so long after my shift that I had to go home, I'd drop by the shop on the way and collect a bottle of wine. Once home, whilst my baby lay asleep upstairs, I'd drink the bottle to help me get to sleep. This continued from weeks into months and you would have had to be blind not to notice that something was wrong with my home life. The Sergeant that I had at the time was of an old-school nature and due to my partner also being a cop, and there being no physical violence, no help was offered and he stayed out of my business.

I had nothing other than my child and my job so I threw myself into being the best mother I could be, taking her to all the mums and tots groups that I could and various play areas and parks. We rarely stayed in the house so I didn't mess it up before he got home. I became savvy at finding free places where me and my child could make memories together. At work, I threw myself into my job and decided to try and be the best police officer I could be. Eventually, there was a clear routine of which shifts I would be working alongside on each day of the month. I showed interest in being involved in the planned policing operations that were ongoing in my area, such as drugs warrants or locating wanted people. Each day I turned up for work and was handed a long list of pre-arranged jobs and statements to take whilst the rest of the team went out and did the planned operations. I became the team bitch. If they didn't want to do one of their jobs, it was handed to me to complete. It was made clear from the outset by the supervisors that I wasn't part of any one team and I was going to be used whilst on duty, to do the jobs that nobody else wanted to do. I didn't at this point have the mental strength to challenge the supervision's decisions and I was still getting paid the same amount, regardless of the task I did so I continued to come in to be the team's bitch.

The day then came when my Sergeant had to complete my annual appraisal. Whilst in the room with this Sergeant, he told me that I was lacking in many areas, that I needed to be "More involved," that I needed to, "Learn my local criminal targets" and that, "You should be doing more with the team". I remained calm but asked how exactly I was expected to complete any of those requirements if I was being given the shit jobs to do every day? I was told that it was my job to put myself forward for jobs and that if my shifts didn't fit with a team, maybe I needed to look at changing them. It was so easy for him to sit there and tell me all that, but he didn't know that my anxiety of leaving my daughter meant that only two people ever cared for her. He knew that my home life was strained but didn't realise that going home and asking my partner to vary his shifts would have caused weeks of verbal abuse and put downs. He sat there and viewed me as an awkward woman, wanting my own way with flexible shifts but didn't understand the half of it. I refused to sign the appraisal and walked out. Even after this conversation, I continued to attend work and nothing changed. I was given the same old jobs as before and without any energy to argue, continued to do these without further complaint.

After a few months of being back at work and building new friendships with colleagues, my confidence started to grow. I attended Domestic Violence jobs where I was advising young women that the behaviour my partner was displaying towards me was a form of abuse and they shouldn't be putting up with it. The next time I was at home and my partner picked on something I hadn't done correctly, I stood up for myself, again he called me a scrounger in his house and I snapped. I told him I was leaving him and never coming back. The abuse and bullying was finally over and I was ready to take control of my own life once again.

With nowhere to go and nobody to turn to, I knew I couldn't just leave there and then. All the furniture in the house was jointly owned and he was never going to let me take anything. I had not long returned to work from maternity leave, so had no savings and at that point I had to plan. I told him that I would be leaving in two months, this was enough time for me to save up enough money for a deposit on a rental property. Those two months were hell. He upped the ante on the threat of social services, he told me that he would tell them that I was mental. He told me that he would change the locks when I went to work so I couldn't get back in afterwards and he would refuse to let me have our daughter. He told me that he would take her out of the country and never return with her. I went to work every day petrified to return home to the locks having been changed or her having been taken. On many occasions, he would leave his keys in the back of the door, meaning I couldn't get in. He would make me stand there knocking on the door, embarrassing myself in front of the neighbours, and only let me in when he had decided I'd been left long enough. I spent the evenings sleeping on the sofa or on the floor next to my daughter's cot, crying myself to sleep.

Exhausted, his verbal abuse worsened. I'd be feeding our daughter and she would be having a fussy day, refusing her food. He would take the spoon from me and tell me I was useless and an unfit mother and proceed to try and do it himself. He reduced me to tears hourly telling me I was mental, he made me believe that I had nothing to offer our child. He made me believe that she would be better off without me. I'd put her to bed and drink alcohol until I was numb. Some nights one bottle of wine just didn't cut it, I was drinking two or three bottles just to sleep.

Eventually I had managed to get through it and saved enough money for a flat for me and my daughter. I had no money for furniture or decoration but I didn't care, I was finally free. I took a very small amount of my daughter's clothes and toys and left.

The bullying continued. This guy is a police officer and you would expect him to be a law-abiding citizen, he was far from it. He knew that he could no longer control me, so started to use my daughter to continue his soul destroying games. I wanted to get as far away from him as possible but he guilt tripped me into thinking that I was in the wrong for moving our daughter out of his house and away from her daddy. As a result, I chose an apartment that was close to his house and his place of work so he could come and see her as often as he needed. I never wanted to come between him and his child and didn't want her to be without her father. On his days off, he would take our child and then refuse to bring her home; he continued to tell me, and anyone that would listen, that I was an unfit mother. He had refused to part with either her birth certificate or passport and continually stated that he was going to take her so far away that I would never see her again. Knowing the law, I knew that he had just as much right to our child as I did and I knew that he didn't require my permission to take her out of the country. I was living my life on a knife edge, never knowing what was going to happen next.

Whilst at work, I confided in a colleague and old friend who often came around to my flat, to check on me and make me go out to the shops and not hide away for days on end. Our relationship grew and he became my new partner. This caused more problems for me. If we were seen out at the local shops or out in the area with my daughter, I'd almost instantly get an abusive text message from her father, asking why this colleague was at my flat or why we were out shopping together. I was being watched and I couldn't do anything at all without it getting back to my ex. Whilst he was on duty, he would drive his police car past my flat, constantly checking up on me and who I was with. I lived with my blinds closed but even that didn't work. He enlisted the help of other officers on his shift to drive past my place and update him on my whereabouts. I was a prisoner in my own home. It all came to a head one day when my new partner, my daughter and I nipped to the local shops. We walked past an on-duty police officer who was friends with my ex and within seconds, I received yet another abusive text. I was exhausted and just about ready to give up. When he took her the next time and yet again refused to bring her home, I went into melt down. I had no fight left in me, so I drew my curtains, locked my front door and drank that much alcohol that I slept. I couldn't cope with my own life, let alone anyone else's problems at work, so, I didn't show up for my shift. I didn't feel suicidal, I just wanted to sleep, to feel numb and forget the sadness that filled my body.

After a few days of refusing to answer my phone, not showing up for work and refusing to answer the door, people became increasingly worried and there was a rather believable threat of my door being forced in. That was enough to get me out of bed and open it. Most of the next few days that followed passed in an emotional blur of people coming around, waking me up, getting me out of bed and then frogmarching me to the doctors. The GP took one look at me and signed me off work for at least 3 months. He prescribed strong anti-depressants and ordered that I refer myself to the occupational health and welfare unit within the police, who offer counselling and such things. I agreed to do anything in my power to get myself back on track and become strong enough to have my daughter home. In the three months that I had off work, I attended regular weekly counselling sessions provided for me free of charge through work. These sessions allowed me to identify that the behaviour which had led me to breaking point was a form of abuse and was in no part my fault. It made me see that after having my daughter I suffered very early on from postnatal depression, due to her poor care in hospital, and alongside that, I had major separation anxiety when it came to my little girl.

Once I had recognised my triggers and difficulties, I became stronger and learned ways to deal with situations that were difficult. During my time off work I received no support from the supervisors and other than wanting to come into my home for a meeting, I heard nothing from them. I felt guilty however for being off work, I felt like a fraud as I hadn't a broken leg or any physical injury, my problem was invisible to anyone else. I felt like people thought I was making it all up. I knew that I would have to get back to work and reintegrate with the shift, so through fear of being treated as a liar, I went back far too early. I spoke with one of my Sergeants and arranged to come back on a day that he was present in the police station so that if I struggled, I could ask for his help. My new partner worked at the same police station and was on duty on the day I returned. His shift had been changed at the last minute by the Inspector to facilitate a last-minute warrant that was to be executed. I felt a little relieved at this as he would be there for added moral support.

The fear of returning was much greater than the reality and when I got back into the swing of things and settled in, it became second nature once again. A week after my return, I was called into the Inspector's office. This female Inspector has got a reputation for being rude and abrupt and very uncaring. As soon as we went into her office and the door was shut, I felt the atmosphere go frosty. It was clear from the offset that she didn't like me very much and by what she was saying, I was a bit of a problem to her given my recent absence for depression. She made it quite clear that she wasn't interested in the slightest in my mental health issues or my personal issues with my ex-partner. It became clear that she was a little pissed off with me and had brought me into her office to make an example of me. She told me that she believed that I was sly and that I had manipulated her Sergeant to change my shift on my first day back. She explained that she knew me and my new partner were in a relationship and that she thought I had changed my shift to work with him. She told me that she didn't buy into my depression and if I was going to last on her shift I better buck up my ideas. I tried to explain to her that I had changed my shift a week in advance, to allow me the support of my supervision and that had she not insisted that my partner change his shift, we would have been on opposite shifts anyway.

She was rude and spoke to me like a piece of dirt, all the anxiety and worry of coming back to work came flooding back and I started to panic. I didn't want her to think that she could bully me in such a cruel way so I began to argue my case. I lost my temper with her and whilst she was stood over me shouting, I stood up and told her that she would benefit from pulling her stuck up head out of her fat arse. She had lost the small amount of respect I had for her, both as an inspector and a person. I was in tears and a shaking mess. I wanted to get out of her office and run home never to return, but I knew that I was supposed to be a cop, a responsible person. I could not let her win, I would not give up again. I sat in the writing room at a computer, staring at the screen with tears rolling down my face, confused about what to do next.

Over the following months, I kept my head down at work, keeping myself constantly busy. I continued to take my anti-depressants and eventually the dark cloud started to lift. My ex still tried to control me but the stronger I got, the less I allowed him.

Eventually, I became pregnant with my son and once again was taken off front-line duties. This time I remained at the same police station on light duties and assisted the team with all the enquiries that could be done from the station. I was told that I was not allowed any face to face contact with the public, to protect my unborn child. This, however, was as and when it suited. If the Inspector couldn't find another officer to take a witness statement or do an errand, I was utilised. When I told her that I wasn't allowed any contact with the public, I was told to stop moaning and do as I was told and go and take the statement. Once again my child didn't want to wait for his due date and six weeks early, he decided to make an appearance.

The birth was horrendous and he was born so quickly that he wasn't breathing. The pain I went through caused me to lose consciousness and stop breathing and during one point, both my son and I were being given oxygen and CPR at the same time. He was quickly whisked away to the neo natal unit and placed in intensive care. He required assistance breathing and was placed on a CPAP ventilator, along with many IV drips. He had an infection and was given intravenous antibiotics and medication. I was left in the hospital delivery suite all alone with my partner. With no baby in my arms, not knowing how he was, it was heart breaking. Eventually, when we were allowed down to see him, he looked so vulnerable and helpless in his incubator. At 5lb 14oz. he was massive compared to the rest of the babies in the ward. This seemed to help him get better much quicker than the nurses expected. When he was three days old, I got to hold him and I cried happy tears for him. I had an overwhelming urge to feed him myself and his tiny body became stronger and fought off the infection quicker than any of the nurses thought he would. This was the same hospital that had made the mistake with my daughter, but this time was completely different. The neo natal nurses at Stepping Hill Hospital were like angels on earth and without them, my son wouldn't be here today. My experience of motherhood this time around was the opposite of the last time. My new partner was the most supportive man on the planet, he was there to assist morning, noon and night and doted on our son unconditionally. Without ever being asked, he treated both my son and my daughter the same and adored both. My life was complete and finally I was happy.

After twelve months on maternity leave, I began thinking

about returning to work. I was contacted by a supervisor two weeks before Christmas and asked which shifts I intended to return on. I explained that I wished to maintain the shifts that I was on before, as they fitted around my ex-partner's shifts and allowed me to sort out childcare and not have to worry about any arguments with him. I was told by the Sergeant that this was probably going to be ok and that he would get back to me if there were any problems. About three days before Christmas, I received a phone call from the female Inspector with whom I had had previous problems. She told me that due to a change on the division, she would not be authorising my flexible working plan. She explained that she would no longer allow me to be on a five-week shift plan and that I needed to resubmit a new shift plan that fitted around her requirements. I panicked, I knew that if I had to go back to my ex-partner and rejig the shifts, it would spark his controlling abusive behaviour again, so I asked her if I could be placed anywhere else in the force. I explained that I would do any job, working at any location. I'd even clean toilets if I had to, but I really needed my shift plan to work around the response officer's shifts. She told me that I was lucky to have a job in the police, working a flexible working plan. She said that no other department would want me as a part time worker on their shift and that I had to resubmit a new plan.

It was two days now before Christmas and I went into panic mode. I was left to worry all over the Christmas period, so on January 2nd I decided to seek more advice on the matter. I rang the central Human Resources department and asked them for their advice. I was told that I could appeal the Inspector's decision and complain that her decision had not been made official, as I had nothing in writing at this stage. I had to write an email, outlining the reasons why I required this specific shift plan. I had to explain what steps I had taken to enable the shift plan to work for the role of a police officer, and I had to explain what conversations had taken place with my Inspector.

I compiled the email and explained that I had received nothing in writing. I explained that I had been left all over the Christmas period, worrying about my future in the police and had even gone to the extent of writing my letter of resignation. I explained that I had offered to work in any other department, in any other location of the force and after being told that nobody would want me, I had made the decision that I needed to look for another job.

The appeal email was supposed to be sent to my Sergeant who in turn had to send it to the Inspector, who was then duty bound to forward it on to the Senior Leadership Team. Well, this is exactly what didn't happen. I sent the email to the Sergeant and he did his job, sending it to the Inspector, but the email stopped there. The process, in my opinion, was corrupt and backwards. The Inspector refused to forward the email to the SLT, stating in her reply to me that I had failed to complete several important steps. She went on to list various things that she said she had told me to do in our telephone conversation, which were all lies. She stated that I was supposed to attend a meeting with her, but this conversation never happened. She said that she had offered to help me, this had never happened. She said that she had in fact, offered support and again, this never happened.

In the end, I decided to seek legal advice from my Police Federation representative. After one meeting with the Federation rep, it was clear that this Inspector had a personal vendetta against me and I was soon moved on to a new shift, with the five-week shift plan which I had requested. The personal issue of this Inspector bullying me was swept well and truly under the carpet, as many complaints about her had been before and have been since.

DEMENTIA

Before I joined the police, I had heard of dementia, however, had never met anyone with it. I just thought it's what makes old people confused and forget things. My first ever experience of dementia was when I was on duty one night, in company with my tutor Chris. He was driving our police car and it was about 3am; we were parked at a cross road junction, quite close to the station. As the lights turned to green, he went to drive across the junction. A car came out of nowhere from the left and almost hit the side of us. The car had clearly jumped a red light, so Chris put on his emergency equipment and went after it in an attempt to pull it over.

Once pulled over at the side of the road, I jumped out of the police car and went to speak to the driver. I came across an elderly man of about 86 years old. He was dressed in his pyjamas and said that he couldn't sleep, so had come for a drive. He apologised profusely and said he had never been stopped by the police in his whole life before. Given the time of night and how shaken up the man was, I decided to use my discretion and issue the man with a producer. That way, he wouldn't receive a fine or points but would have to attend a police station and produce his full driving licence, MOT and insurance. He was given his producer and went on his way. Two weeks later, I received a notice that told me the man had failed to attend the police station and produce his documents.

I had his address, so I went around to see him in my full

police uniform. He answered the door and looked at me as if he had never seen me before. He was polite and invited me in; as I walked into his living room, all the signs were there. Post-it notes were pinned everywhere, on the walls, doors and mirrors, all reminding him of different tasks he needed to do throughout the day, including the simplest things such as eat breakfast or have a wash. The penny dropped and I realised that this man hadn't intentionally failed to produce his documents, he had simply forgotten. At that point, there was no way I would even dream of prosecuting him. I did know that I had to do something though. He was clearly unfit to drive a car if he couldn't remember basic tasks, so I began to ask the man about his family. I located a number for his son and when I was safely back in my car, out of earshot, I made the call. I explained exactly why I was contacting him and he explained that his father had dementia. I asked why he still had access to his car and he said that so far, he hadn't found the spare key which his father was using. I explained that I was going to apply to the DVLA to have his licence revoked for his own safety, and the whole family agreed with me. I was told that they had put it off for so long as his car was his very last bit of independence and without it, they feared that he would be trapped at home alone. I explained my reasons, confiscated the man's keys and the DVLA revoked his licence.

Approximately four weeks later, I was sent to a sudden death at an address I recognised. It turned out to be the same gentleman's house. I was so upset and felt awful that taking the licence from him had, in my opinion, allowed him to give up. However, it was the only option I had.

Throughout my career dementia has featured in many jobs, particularly in jobs where elderly people have wandered out of their homes or care homes. Once it had been noticed that they had gone off alone, the police were called and a huge hunt for them began. Many of the missing people had varying degrees of dementia, from just simply being a little forgetful of their own addresses, to not even knowing their own name or the name or faces of others.

I remember one lady who was a bugger for getting out in the middle of the night. Luckily she and her husband lived close to the police station and whilst driving about in the small hours, I would spot her walking along in the direction of the town centre shops. I knew her by name and would always stop for a chat. I knew if I spoke to her I could always cheer her up and make sure I didn't confuse or fluster her. She would always be adamant that she was going shopping, but I always managed to convince her to get in my car so I could take her home.

Another lady I remember had been with her husband for over 60 years. They had been inseparable and now both in their eighties, she had developed dementia. Her husband was of sound mind but was frail and struggled with his mobility. Their children had tried to convince them to move to sheltered accommodation where they could be properly cared for, but their father was stubborn and adamant that he could care for his wife alone, as it was his job. One morning, the lady left the house whilst the man was in bed. He awoke at lunch time to find her missing and hadn't a clue where she had gone, or what time she had left. He left it for a few hours, hoping that she would return, but when it became dark and she still wasn't home, he raised the alarm. This is a hard job to deal with for a cop. With no idea what time she left, no idea if she had taken any cash and completely no idea of what she may have been wearing, it was like finding a needle in a haystack. Immediately, a report of a missing lady was put out to all CCTV operators, bus depots and neighbouring divisions and forces. The weather had become poor and cold, the worry and risk level was increasing by the second. I just kept thinking that this lady was someone's wife, mum and grandma, and we needed to find her safe and well. Luckily, the lady had walked approximately 15 miles in only her slippers and house coat and had gone back to an address where she lived as a child. She had failed to knock on the door and had just walked in, scaring the occupants to death. The lady had been out all day and was soaking and covered in mud. Her slippers were torn and her feet were all cut and bruised. She had also soiled herself. The residents had contacted their local police office who had dispatched two officers to go and help. On their way, they had been told of the job on our force and managed to bring her safely home. It broke my heart seeing her in that way and I felt awful for her family, to have to see their loved one in such a manner. I hoped that I would never have to experience such a horrific illness. Unfortunately, life is cruel and my nanna developed the disease.

When I was a little girl, I was mainly brought up by au pairs and my nanna Alice. The au pairs were foreign students who wanted to come over to England to study and learn English. They lived in our spare room and I doubt that they knew what was in store for them before they set off for sunny England. For a very small wage, they had to do an awful lot. They had to get me and my sisters up every morning and get us dressed and fed. They had to get us to school, then themselves to their English course. They would have to be back in time to collect us from school, make our tea, bath us, do the washing and ironing and tidy the house. On their days off, my nan would come and take care of us. She was a pain in the arse as she was so strict. She wouldn't let us play out and made us go to bed at 6.30pm, even at the age of ten. I used to lie in my room and listen to all my friends still playing out in the street outside.

Every weekend or during the school holidays, my nan would take us on adventures. She would often take us to Castleton in Derbyshire. Here, we would park up in a carpark at the bottom of Mam Tor, and walk up the hundreds of steps to the top of the hill that we thought was an actual mountain. She would then walk us down into Castleton and we would play on a park or have an ice cream. When we were ready to leave, she would walk us up the 'shivering mountain' (it was part of the hill where, due to the movement of the land, the road had crumbled and collapsed) and back up to the carpark.

Her job was as a carer and she often went to Wrexham to care for an elderly blind man. We would go with her and spent many days exploring places, in and around the Welsh coast. I fondly remember her taking us to Blackpool and giving us each some 2ps for the slot machines, and then buying us fish and chips which we ate on the front.

I remember looking forward to sleep-overs at her flat because we would camp out on the living room floor. She would take me to the local co-op and buy me hot chicken wings and a jar of cockles. She was the best nanna and cared for us in the only way she knew how. She was strict and we did get punched in the arm if we misbehaved but I loved her more than anything on the planet.

As I grew up, I'd always go and visit her and if I ever had any news, she would be the first I'd tell. When I was pregnant with each of my children, I went straight to my nan and told her first. When they were born, she was one of the first to hold them. She has always been, and will always be, a massive part of my world.

Approximately four years ago, my nan became ill. She started losing weight and we established that she had stopped eating. When I went to see her, she seemed confused. She couldn't remember the small things, like birthdays and special occasions. I used to think that was normal for old people to become forgetful, but when she began to forget to put in her teeth and forget to eat, we became concerned. She was tested for dementia and given an MRI scan to see how bad it was. The results came back that she was suffering from early onset of Vascular Dementia. I had googled dementia and all the negative things showed up in the search engine including the fact that it was degenerative and incurable. I was devastated.

Slowly, over the months and years that followed, my nan started to deteriorate. She forgot how to cook for herself, so we booked her meals on wheels which she hated. She started to either forget to take her medication, or take too much. We all clubbed together and checked on her daily until social services became involved. They assessed her and decided that she needed carers. We got her a safe to put her medication in, so the carers could administer it and so that she wouldn't overdose again.

She forgot how to bath herself, and how to get dressed. Her cognitive thought process had completely broken down.

One morning when I visited, her eye looked sore. I asked a doctor to come and check on her but they couldn't get her an appointment, so I went and picked her up and took her to the doctors myself. They eventually agreed to see her and said she had conjunctivitis. She needed the medication to be administered four times a day, but the carers only attended twice a day so, at lunch time between my classes, I went around.

When I arrived at her flat, she didn't let me in and I panicked. I used the key safe to let myself in and found her sleeping on the sofa. I woke her up and started to make her lunch and a coffee before going to bathe her eye. She looked confused and started to ask if I was her carer. I said, "No nanna, it's me," but still she insisted I was a carer. I knew the day would come where she forgot who I was, but I didn't expect it to be so soon. I felt winded like someone had punched me in the stomach, and wanted to cry. I didn't break until I had left her flat, as I didn't want her to become upset.

I sat in my car and cried, I felt like I had lost my nan. My mum and I have a very strained relationship and I hadn't seen her for almost a year, but I felt the need to talk to her and tell her how bad my nan was. My mum is my nanna's main carer, so communication was a necessity, but we did this via text message. It was the first time I had spoken to her in almost twelve months, and I sat there and sobbed on the phone. It took me a few days to readjust, and I went to see my nan every day. I began to realise that, despite her not remembering me, she was happy. She was in a different world now, where everyone she met was like a stranger, but she was happy in her world.

When it was decided that carers would be doing all her personal care, I stepped in. This woman had spent her entire life caring for others, including me. I felt it was my time to step up and care for her. I had a full-time job and two small children, so she still required daily carers; however, I attended to bath her and wash and dry her hair for her. At first, it felt really uncomfortable and I didn't know how to give her the independence and privacy, but still assist her into and out of the bath, but after a few times we got into our routine. When I care for her now, I do it like I would for my children. I sit and massage her shoulders and remind her of the good times we had.

I remembered seeing a man on Facebook who played music to his father whilst they were in the car. The story said that his father had dementia and when the music was played, he became alive and started singing along, remembering all the words. I decided to give it a try with my nan. I found some music from the 1940s on YouTube and started to play it for her. The result was unreal, I sat and cried watching her dance around the living room and sing along, getting all the words exactly right. This lady, who is my world, had forgotten me, forgotten many details of her past and present but was stood before me, happy as I'd ever seen her.

I began to play her music when she was in the bath, and it seemed to spark a cognitive memory of how to get herself out. I researched buying her a music player and eventually I found one specifically designed for dementia. My mum bought it for her and now she has her favourite tunes at her fingertips, all day long. I cannot believe the power that music had on my nanna.

I took her to the 2016 Walk to Remember in Heaton Park,

Manchester. I was amazed at how many people turned up. Thousands and thousands of people joined the walk, all raising money for such an amazing cause. I pushed my nan around the route whilst she waved to everyone like she was royalty and genuinely thought all the people had attended just to see her. It made me smile.

I go and see my nanna often and each time, deep down, I'm petrified that I'll find her dead. I'm hoping that she has lots of happy years left.

Dementia is a cruel disease. I hope one day a cure is found as I wouldn't wish anyone to watch their loved one slowly fade away.

DEATH / SUICIDE / MURDER

At the ripe old age of 18½, I had experienced most things you'd expect a 40-year-old to have done. I had lived a colourful life and was not behind the door when it came to dealing with real life, and what living alone from a young age allowed you to experience. However, coming from relatively young parents, I had never experienced death, or the loss of someone close. Deep down the thought terrified me; however, never one to turn my back on a challenge, I decided to face my fear head on.

During my probationary police training period, I arranged a visit to the local hospital mortuary, near to where I was going to be stationed. In the old days "Life on Mars times" as a probationer, you were forced to attend and stay through a whole post mortem. When I joined, this wasn't the case anymore and if you wanted to attend one, you had to get permission from the Coroners Liaison Officer first. So I did exactly that: me and two of the colleagues who I joined with, attended the morgue on a cold, Wednesday morning.

Driving up to the hospital, I had total panic building up in me. It went from my stomach, into my chest and I couldn't stop it. As I parked up, I put on a brave face for my colleagues and we walked up the path to the morgue. The building was large and grey and quite non-descript. The smell was one I had not experienced before but reminded me of cleanliness; it wasn't bad or unpleasant, which I had assumed it would be. We rang the bell and were greeted by a jolly man with short, grey hair, wearing a smart suit and tie. He introduced himself as the Coroner Liaison Officer. We were taken to a small office that housed a small desk and one small computer. The wall to the left was a retractable partition wall, which reminded me of the ones that we used to have in the school assembly hall. We had a short discussion about the role of a Coroner Liaison Officer, and what they expect from police officers when they attend any types of death. After being sat in the small office for approximately ten minutes, the Coroner Liaison Officer asked if we were ready to experience our first dead body. Trying to maintain my calm, brave exterior I said "YES". He stood up and pulled back the retractable wall and there lay a man on a bed, covered up to his neck in a white sheet. He had been there behind the partition wall the whole time we were sat there, less than 6ft away. A wave of emotions passed over me. He was barely a man, mid-twenties. He lay so still, no life left in him, his eyes closed, he just looked simply asleep. His complexion was pale, but not like you see in the movies, he didn't look like I assumed a dead person would look, he just looked peaceful.

I then began to think about this man and his life, the fact that he may be someone's husband, brother, father or son. The fact that he was so young, far too young to die. I began to wonder how he died, as he had no marks or bruises, and then I felt sad for his poor lost soul.

After this, the Coroner Liaison Officer showed us into part of the mortuary where all the bodies were stored. It smelled really clinical, a strange, unusual clean smell. The Liaison Officer opened the door of what looked like a huge refrigerator; inside were trays and trays of dead bodies, all being kept cold and fresh, ready for their funerals or post mortems. It all just seemed so cold and impersonal. It made me sad. The staff that worked there were brilliant though. When I told them about feeling sad at how cold and impersonal it all felt, they offered up a big, beaming smile and told me that they treat every single person as if they were still alive. They said that whilst they are dealing with them, they talk to them, calling them by their name and treating them like a personal family member. This made me smile and made me feel a little brighter. The whole experience of death on the day left me feeling like it was completely clinical and peaceful and like I could easily go and deal with it professionally whilst I was out on duty, without being scared. I felt that now, I could give the family of the deceased a good service and treat the deceased with the respect and dignity they deserved.

This leads me on to being out in company with my tutor constable. You are in company with a tutor constable for 10 weeks. This is broken down into two five week sections, with a different tutor each time. For the sake of this book, I'll call my first tutor Chris and second Smithy. Both tutors were totally different, like chalk and cheese.

The first sudden death I ever attended was with Chris. I'd been on the streets for about two weeks when we were called to a small block of flats in our area. On the drive there, I felt really nervous again. I wanted to impress my tutor, so in my head I was going through what I was supposed to do and say when I arrived there. I repeated the steps in my head:

1. Introduce myself and offer condolences
2. Explain that I'm not there acting as a police officer, but as a representative of the coroner
3. Check the circumstances surrounding the death
4. Search the body manually for any injuries, or signs of any foul play
5. Place a bracelet around their wrist with all the personal details on for the undertaker (check this twice, as you would get an ass-kicking off the undertaker if the spelling was wrong)
6. Take an identification statement
7. Fill in a death report

8. Contact the undertaker
9. Wait until the undertaker arrives

On our arrival, we already knew what we were going to. The radio operator had informed us that the deceased person was in her eighties, she had been quite poorly and her death was expected by her family. Her family were at the address we were going to, which is always good, as it means we do not have to attempt to find any next of kin.

My tutor looked at me, asking if I was ready to go and deal with it and I told him I was. My voice said yes; however, my head was saying no. As we entered the flat, I expected to be greeted by upset relatives; however, it was quite the opposite. I found four people having a good old chin wag in the living room, whilst the lady's husband was busying himself in the kitchen brewing up. I took the lead after a little shove from my tutor, introducing us both. After all the formalities, I asked politely if I could see Lilly, the lady who had died. Expecting to be shown into the bedroom, her husband looked at me in a confused, bewildered manner. He pointed to a lady on the sofa who I had assumed was asleep. She was sat at the end of the sofa, surrounded by the other three people who were deep in discussion when we had arrived. It totally threw me and I couldn't speak. I froze. I didn't understand how they could all be sat around poor Lilly, so calmly chatting like it was normal to be in the same room as a dead lady, especially a loved one. My tutor had to take over as my mind went blank, and he filled in the death report and did the statement for me. He, and all Lilly's family, left the room whilst I conducted the manual, physical search of her body. I was petrified, I felt like running and not turning back but I took a deep breath and began. Firstly, I put on some latex gloves and then began my search. Lilly was cold; her skin was like ice and that alone felt strange. Rigor mortis had set in and she was completely stiff and difficult to move; despite her eyes being shut, I felt like she was watching me the entire time. I felt like I was invading her personal space, it felt like I was violating her privacy, this was totally uncomfortable and alien to me. As I leaned Lilly forwards to check for any injuries to the back of her head or back, a strange dull groan sound came from her chest. I have never been so scared in my life and jumped out of my skin. I was on the verge of tears, and I must have made some kind of animalistic shriek because Chris shot into the living room to check on us. I was trying to remain professional, but I was stood a foot away from Lilly, who was now lay bent double on the sofa. I just remember that I kept repeating "SHE MADE A NOISE! SHE BREATHED". Chris sat Lilly back up and made her presentable, he placed the bracelet that I was holding onto, around her wrist. He then ordered me out of the flat and told me to wait in the police car for him. I didn't even attempt to argue, I left the flat as quickly as I could and headed to the safety of the car.

Approximately 10 minutes later, Chris emerged from the block of flats and got into the driver's seat. He looked at me with a serious face and I thought I was going to get a telling off, but a second later he was laughing uncontrollably at me, tears in his eyes. Through hysterics he tried to explain that when you move a person who has died, sometimes a build-up of gases leaves their body, which is what made the sound. However, this was a sharp introduction to the banter on the shift. Chris revelled in telling the rest of the shift about what had happened, trying to copy the primal, petrified noise I had made. The rest of the shift ribbed me for the next few days. It didn't upset me though. It kind of made a situation that was difficult much easier to deal with. At twenty years old, I had now dealt with my first ever death as a police officer.

The fear of death hadn't left me yet though, so I made it my business to volunteer for as many jobs of this nature as possible.

The next week, a police call taker took a call from an extremely upset young man. He told them that he had attended his dad's house to check on him but when he went inside, he couldn't find him until he tried the bathroom door. He told the call taker that he had found his dad on the floor in the bathroom, blocking the door and that he had died. Me and Chris were given this job and told it was on a grade 1; which meant we were to use the blue lights and sirens to get there as quickly as we safely could. It felt like we were there in a matter of seconds; however, it was really a few minutes. When we arrived, we knocked on the door and received no answer which was confusing, as the man who made the call said he was waiting for us. We double-checked the address with the radio operator, who confirmed we were in the right place. We knocked again, this time a real loud police man's knock, but still received no answer. This made the next-door neighbour come out. She told us that she had just seen the elderly gentleman and his son get into the rear of an ambulance which sped off with its lights and sirens on. I could see the panic in Chris's face. If someone dies and it is unexplained, then nobody should move the body until police arrive. The paramedics and ambulance service are well aware of this. Chris requested that the radio operator contact the hospital and ambulance control room. After about five long, worrying minutes we were finally updated on what had actually happened at the house.

The homeowner's son had arrived to check on his dad, finding him on the floor in the bathroom, he'd automatically assumed the worst that his father had died. He had done this without physically checking him and in a blind panic, had rung the police. Before Chris and I were dispatched to the job, an ambulance had been contacted by the police call taker. The ambulance arrived before us and upon examination of the elderly male, he was very much still alive and kicking. He had suffered a stroke, causing him to fall on the bathroom floor, breathing but unconscious. The paramedics rushed him straight off in the ambulance to the local A and E department, where he was booked in and finally made a full recovery. Upon mine and Chris's arrival at the house it appeared, on the face of it, that we had lost a dead man. Thank God we were wrong.

These were the deaths that were called in by the families, of persons who had only just died in the past hour or two. The next set of five weeks I did, with my tutor Smithy, were set to be a lot more testing. The title of the jobs changed slightly and I had a sharp introduction to the "CONCERN FOR WELFARE" jobs in the queue.

The main job in my probation that will always stay etched in my memory is my first concern for welfare. When I think back, I can remember the smell, the feeling and the terrible scene.

Smithy, on our way to the job, was winding me up and telling me tales of gruesome dead bodies. He had been in the job for over 20 years, so had seen his fair share. He kept telling me that he was sending me in first to check it out, and as the probationer I had to do as he said. By the time we arrived I was a quivering mess. The radio operator had told us that the call had come in from a concerned neighbour who had noticed the post spilling out of her neighbour's letter box, and milk bottles stacked up untouched on the door step.

On our arrival, we knocked on the front door and got no answer. I spoke to the occupant's neighbour and established that the occupant was a lone female who lived in the upstairs flat. She was in her fifties and kept herself to herself. She rarely had visitors and when she did, she never invited them in, she kept them talking outside on the doorstep. We also found out that she kept a small dog who was her best friend, and she cared very well for it. This was the only thing she had for company, as she didn't have any friends. The elderly neighbour said that she hadn't seen or heard from her in a while, but that didn't surprise me as I was stood right in front of her, and she was as deaf as a door post and couldn't hear a word I was saying.

Smithy had been speaking to other neighbours, and found

out that the lady in the flat had caused a few problems on the Close in recent months. She had been sneaking out in the early hours, and had been stealing bin bags full of rubbish from her neighbour's bins. In doing so, it appeared that she had left the Close in a mess, and the residents had challenged her over this. When she knew that they were mad about the rubbish, she closed her door and refused to answer any other calls for the rest of the week, which is why no one noticed that she hadn't been out in a while. Smithy had already checked the lady, who we now knew was called Susan, hadn't been admitted to the local hospitals and it had come back as a negative, she had not been admitted or hadn't even visited them.

As police officers, I quickly learned that we only force entry to a house i.e. 'put the door in' if we have an honest belief that there is someone inside that needs our help, so to save "LIFE AND LIMB" or as a last resort after checking hospitals and any relatives.

Anyhow, all checks had been done and so we went back to the front door. Looking through the glass, I could see a net curtain obstructing my view. I bent down and posted a long stick through the letter box to move the curtain and as I did, about twenty bluebottle flies flew out of the letterbox, hitting me in the face. The smell through the letterbox was vile, it was not like anything I had ever experienced before. I'd describe it as a mixture of rotting rubbish, rotting meat and urine all mixed together, it was vile. Now I had disturbed the net curtain, flies swarmed around the inside of the glass. These were not normal flies, they were huge, buzzing bluebottles that wouldn't have looked out of place with tattoos on their arms and jockeys on their backs.

Smithy confirmed my thoughts and seriously told me to expect the worse, my heart sank. He told me that he genuinely thought that Susan had died inside and from the flies and smell, he believed that she had been there for some time. Smithy went to fetch the wham ram which is the big, red, heavy, metal implement the police used to break down doors. Normally after a couple of strikes, the doors collapse and go in easily; however, this door seemed to be jammed on something. As Smithy hit it for the final time, I heard the door keys drop out of the inside of the lock. The door burst open and we were in. At that moment an army of beastly bluebottle super flies flew out right at us, desperate for their freedom. The smell hit me, it was unbearable, stronger than ever; my eyes began to water.

The keys dropping on the inside of the door assured me that Susan was definitely in the flat as there was only one door in and out, and we were stood at it. As I braved climbing the stairs of the first floor flat, there were approximately 20–30 bin bags of rotting rubbish on them. They were torn and split and spilling out all over the floor. I was trying to be brave and professional, but the smell was overwhelming, making my eyes water and my gut wretch. As I got to the top of the stairs, I noticed that the floor, walls and ceiling were moving. On closer inspection, millions of tiny maggots and insects were forming a carpet on the floor and walls. They were dropping on me from the ceiling, it was like something out of a horror film and that's when I felt my stomach go, I clambered back down the stairs as quickly as I could before knocking Smithy clean over. As soon as I cleared the front door, I threw up in the bush close by. As I turned around I had a sea of worried, upset faces looking at me. It was just my luck that all the bloody neighbours had come out to see what the commotion was about! One of the neighbours approached me, when he thought he was safe from being puked on. He asked if Susan was dead and to my embarrassment, I had to tell him that as yet I didn't actually know.

With all these eyes on me, I felt it my duty to go back inside with Smithy. The police uniform, at this time, was a white shirt, black trousers and a cravat for us female bobbies. I took off my cravat and unbuttoned the top button of my shirt. When I was out of sight of the neighbours I pulled up my shirt to cover my mouth, ears and nose. I soooo didn't want anything going in or up them. I braved the climb up the stairs once again and found Smithy still at the top of the stairs.

I noticed that despite the flat being quite small it had four rooms, each room except from the bedroom was inaccessible. I'm 5ft 4 tall and each room was piled high with rotting bin bags up to my shoulder height. I was still retching when Smithy brought me back down to earth, and told me that he had found a small dog in the bedroom, still alive. He told me that he thought that the dog was standing on the bed, but this was also covered in rotting rubbish. Smithy had been trying to coax the dog out of the room, but was having no such luck. The poor dog looked emaciated, it was in a really bad way; it appeared very weak and looked to have stitches in its stomach. I went back down the stairs and after a bit of persuasion, managed to get one of the neighbours to part with some meat, to enable me to coax the poor dog out. As soon as I got to the top of the stairs the poor dog jumped on me, devoured the meat and allowed me to carry it outside, where another kind neighbour agreed to take it in and care for it until we had finished.

Once again I braved those dreaded stairs, climbing over rubbish whilst weird insects were dropping on me. As I got to the top of the stairs, there was no sign of Smithy. He had clambered over the mounds of rubbish and insects, and made his way to the bedroom. I found him stood on the bed, looking between the bed and the wardrobe. He called me to come over, so I started and he told me that he had found Susan. It transpired that Susan had slipped on some of the rubbish and had become wedged tightly between the wardrobe and the bed. It also appeared that she had possibly choked on her tongue. It was clear by looking at her legs and stomach, that the small dog had survived by feeding on her. Despite only being there for a maximum of three weeks, Susan's body was badly decomposed. I believe that by hoarding all the rubbish and having all the maggots and insects, it had speeded up the decaying process, turning the majority of Susan's body to mush. This was, and still is, the worst scene I have ever witnessed in my life.

Smithy, thinking he was funny with his sick sense of humour, pointed to Susan's stomach, which was filled with maggots, and told me that they were baby flies and that's where all the flies were coming from. I couldn't get out of the flat fast enough. I practically slipped and stumbled down the stairs and once again, threw up in that well-placed bush. Once I was done, I turned around and faced the swarm of gazing eyes of the residents and, in the most professional way you can with sick dripping down your chin and eyes streaming, gave them the news that we had found Susan, and she had in fact died.

Smithy came out after me and with a side step of my vomit pile, he sprang into action and took charge. Relief swept over me, he informed the radio operator of our discovery and asked for Supervision and CID to attend. He requested an undertaker and Environmental Health. We were in a small Close, so when everyone arrived, it looked like the circus was in town. CID and supervision arrived and got to the front door. Once the smell hit them, they made the decision to tactically withdraw and take mine and Smithy's evidence, rather than going in themselves.

There was then the small matter of the undertakers arriving to remove Susan's body. I stood silently and witnessed one of the weirdest arguments between two professional men in my whole life. Smithy was acting as a referee between the undertaker, Bob and the Environmental Health man, Steve. Bob was telling Steve that they were categorically 100% not entering the flat to remove the body of Susan, until a clear path was made to her body for health and safety reasons. Steve was telling Bob that he and his staff were categorically 100% not entering the flat to clear any path to anything, until the body had been removed, again for their own health and safety reasons. I felt like we were in limbo and nobody was going to use their common sense in this bizarre situation. Even as a newbie, I knew that this situation was ridiculous and nobody was backing down, so I slid off unnoticed, back to the police car. In the boot, I located a full forensic suit, made out of the thin paper type material. I put it on over my already heavily soiled uniform, only so I could cover my ears with the hood. I wasn't risking a maggot or fly in my ear now Smithy had told me where they had come from! I put the mask on and walked over to the squabbling idiots that consisted of the undertaker and the Environmental Health guy. I pretended to be confident and told Steve to lend me a shovel and possibly some fly spray for the bugs. He took one look at me and clearly didn't know what to say or do, so did as he was told and located me a shovel. He brought me a cool bug-killing bomb which I let off at the top of the stairs. Thirty minutes later Smithy and I were suited and booted, shovelling shit in an attempt to clear a path to Susan's body. The smell was unbearable but my stomach was now empty so we continued. Approximately one hour later supervision arrived to assess the scene and arrange for a shift to take over.

When the new supervisor arrived, he was gobsmacked and mortified by what me and Smithy had been left to do. He ordered us to stop straight away and stated that we were not paid to do what we had been doing. We explained the predicament and he agreed that we had done a good job, but stated that there were specialist companies that could attend in full bio-hazard gear to do the same job, without risk of infection or injury. He ordered us to go back to the station and retire from duty.

I remember going home that night and being desperate to get my uniform off. My skin felt like it had maggots crawling all over it. My hair felt like it had bugs and maggots in it. I felt disgusting. After my fifth shower, I began to feel a little better, but I just couldn't shift the smell; it was on my skin, in my hair and under my nails. It just lingered for days despite the constant showers and body spray. My fella saw how exhausted I was when I got home from work, so ordered us a takeout. When it arrived and I saw the rice and noodles, I just saw the maggots all over Susan's body in my mind and legged it to the toilet and threw up again. It was a while before I could stomach eating rice again!

Back on shift the next day, I was the centre of attention. Everyone wanted to know all the gory details. It turns out that poor Susan was the worst death that we have had in our area for over ten years. When the undertakers eventually went in to remove her body, she broke apart and half of her head remained stuck to the bedroom floor. Cops are intrigued about the details I think mainly to mentally prepare for if they ever have to deal with anything as bad.

I learned quickly that cops have a very dark sense of humour. This isn't intended to be disrespectful to the people who had died, or to their family members, but it's a way of dealing with the most horrific incidents and scenes they have to witness.

So with only one week left of my tutor period, I was back in company with Chris. We were called to another, "CONCERN FOR WELFARE".

This job had been reported to the police by a local authority housing association workman. He had attended a block of flats in the area to a report of a leak in a ground floor flat's kitchen ceiling. The workman stated that he had tried knocking at the flat upstairs, but had received no answer and was reporting a strange smell emitting from the flat. On our arrival, I saw that the flats were a ground floor flat with another flat above them. To reach the first floor flats we had to climb an external set of stairs that lead to an external balcony. As soon as I got to the top of the stairs, the smell hit me. It was a smell that will be with me forever, it was the smell of death. I knew in that moment, deep in my gut, that the guy in the upstairs flat had died and had been there for some time, so would be in a bad way. My heart sank.

I looked at Chris and he looked at me and we both mentally prepared ourselves for what we were about to deal with. The flat in question was actually three flats down from the stairs so that gives you an idea of the strength of the smell. As I approached the door, those tell-tale monster bluebottles were buzzing around all the windows. There was no need to do all the usual checks, the signs were all there that this resident had died. Chris went and got the wham ram. I established that the resident was male but all his neighbours didn't really know very much about him, as he kept himself to himself. Chris returned with the wham ram and started to try and force the door. It was a housing association door, which are renowned for being thick, well-made doors that are almost impossible to break into. We requested the housing association handyman to return and drill the locks, which he did. However, it didn't work and we still couldn't get into the flat. It was like Fort Knox! About twenty minutes after the lock smith had tried to force the locks, a very sweaty, red-faced Chris had admitted defeat and asked if the Tactical Aid Unit could attend the flat. The tactical aid team are generally made up of a van load of big, burly men with the odd big burly lady. They have more specialised equipment and are trained to a higher standard at forcing entry to properties. When they arrived, it still took them a good twenty minutes between them, to force the door open. Eventually it broke down. When it did, those big, burly men all turned into scared little girls, screaming and shrieking and flapping away at the swarm of bluebottles that flew out of the door into their faces. As inappropriate as it probably was, given the situation, I couldn't help but laugh.

By this time the Sergeant had arrived at the scene. The Tactical Aid Unit made a quick retreat, and it was our turn to go inside to establish if the resident was still alive or not. We knew that the bloke would be in there deceased, so the Sergeant, my tutor and I flipped a coin to see who was going in first. It had started to get dark outside and the man's electric had gone off and wasn't working. The Sergeant 'Lordy' lost the coin flip and made his way inside by torch light. He must have been inside for literally thirty seconds when he came bounding out of the front door being sick. When he had done, he turned to us and told us that he had found the bloke deceased inside. It appeared that he had fallen out of his bed and was lying face down, naked on his bedroom floor.

The next thing to do was to contact an ambulance because unless a person has been decapitated, the coroner wants a medical professional to attend and pronounce life extinct. Whilst we were waiting, me and Chris went inside the flat to open some windows and the curtains for the faint street lights outside. I went into the bedroom and saw the male face down on the floor, he must have been about 25 stone and he had been in this position for a long time. I knew this because all the fluid in his body had pooled beneath him and the acid from his stomach had started to burn and eat though his skin, causing his body to turn to liquid. I mentally mapped out his flat and the rooms in relation to the flat below, a light bulb came on in my head. The original call came from the maintenance man who had been called out for a leak in the kitchen ceiling of the flat below. When we arrived, there weren't any taps left on in the upstairs flat and I felt sick. I realised that the leak which had been dripping through their ceiling into their cornflakes was in fact this man's decaying body! My stomach flipped and I managed to clear the front door before I threw up all over the Sergeant's newly polished boots.

One job more recently that really made me feel sad was when we were called to yet another concern for welfare. Another patrol had arrived first and it had been decided that we were going to force open the door. The first officer did not like dealing with death, so I offered to take over from him as it now intrigued me. When the door was forced open, we made our way through the tell-tale bluebottles and entered a house that looked to be from the dark ages. There was no electric and no central heating. The rooms were filled with clutter and the floor was covered with what looked to be clothes and materials. There wasn't an inch of floor to be seen. The tell-tale smell of death emitted from every room. The house was dark as all the curtains were drawn, I had to watch my step because there were bits of tissues dotted about with faeces on them and soiled underwear. I couldn't for the life of me find the male resident that we were looking for. I had been in the kitchen, the living room, the bedrooms and the bathroom but I couldn't find anyone. The other officers left the house and something in my gut told me to look again in the living room. I saw a shoe pointing upwards under the clothes, then a leg, then a body and found the man between the TV stand and the wall. He had earlier just blended in with the clothes that were piled high on the floor. Once I had moved the clothes, it appeared that the man had been there for quite some time. He was completely stiff and had mould growing on his hands and neck.

Due to the manner in which I had found him, it looked like he had fallen and as such, I had to request a CID officer and Detective Inspector. When the DI arrived, he went inside and declared that a path needed clearing around the deceased male in order for him to establish if there were any suspicious circumstances. The DI asked me to stand outside and then rolled up his sleeves. With the help of the male CID officer, he moved the sofa on its side and cleared the entire room. He did more graft at this one job than I've seen most DIs do in their career, and not once did he delegate the rubbish, hard jobs to lower ranking officers. I had never met him before, but he had automatically earned my respect and proved that again, there are some officers of all ranks that are still worth their weight in gold. It turned out that the man had just fallen and died where he lay and there were not any suspicious circumstances. The poor guy didn't have any friends or family so was all alone with nobody to notice that he had died.

Another similar job was when a carer had gone in to check

on an elderly gentleman and found him in his bed, where he had died. Again, when I arrived and went inside, there was no electricity and it was late December so it was freezing. The house had never been rewired and had no central heating. The house was tidy and everything looked like it had its place. The dust, however, was thick. The fridge contained enough food for one person for one day. The bedroom in which the man slept was basic, it had a bed with a single blanket and a wardrobe and not much else. When the man was taken by the undertakers, I checked under his mattress as this is where the elderly have a stash of money, and located a few thousand pounds in notes. I then located, in the kitchen drawer, two paying-in books. Each book had approximately £250,000 in each account. I was shocked that this man could live alone in such poverty, but have had access to so much money. I took all the cash I found back to the station and counted it there, with other officers present, and the notes alone came to about £15,000. It just goes to show you that money isn't everything. He was clearly alone and didn't have many family or visitors and chose to live in the way he did.

What really makes me sad about the few deaths that I have just explained is the loneliness these people must have felt. Nobody had visited them for months, nobody cared enough to check on them, nobody even knew they had died. Their neighbours hadn't noticed, their families or relatives hadn't bothered, they were both totally alone. Both people were known to adult social services as being vulnerable people and even they hadn't noticed.

After jobs like these, I go home and hug my family a little bit tighter and promise myself that I will check on my nan every few days, and make sure she is safe and knows she is loved.

So, after an eventful period of being in company with my tutor constables, I made the decision that I was now 100% comfortable with dealing with death. Once on duty on my own, I would often get called to take over from officers who didn't like death. I decided that I was no longer scared of the unknown. I felt I could deal with jobs in an empathetic, professional manner and deal with the families and relatives in the most respectful way possible. I felt like nothing could bother me emotionally anymore... HOW WRONG WAS I? I hadn't experienced suicide before, now this was a whole different ball game.

SUICIDE

The first suicide I ever attended was when I had passed my probationary period and was out on duty on my own. I was told by the radio operator that a gentleman had contacted the police to inform us that his wife, Suranne, had taken her own life.

En route to the job, I expected to find some kind of blood bath in a run-down house. I couldn't have been more wrong. As I pulled up to a beautiful, white cottage, surrounded by beautiful, well-kept gardens and a white picket fence, I felt confused and double-checked with the radio operator that I was in the right place. It was the correct address, so I got out of my car and made my way up the beautiful, cobbled path. Before I could knock I was greeted by a very well-spoken gentleman who wouldn't have looked out of place in Downton Abbey. He looked to be in his fifties and greeted me with a warm and welcoming smile and handshake, and invited me inside, ushering me in the direction of the kitchen. Here, I was greeted by another, younger man who was also very well dressed, well-spoken and was sporting the same warm, welcoming smile. They gestured for me to sit down and offered me a warm drink which I politely declined. I was totally baffled at the entire situation and even asked the man if I was actually in the correct address. The older gentleman introduced himself as Mick and began to explain.

I was twenty years old and this was one of the saddest heart-wrenching stories I had ever heard. Suranne had been a nurse for many years and at the tail end of her nursing career she had been a Macmillan nurse, caring for terminally ill cancer patients; making their end of life as peaceful, pain free and dignified as it could be for both patient and family. In a cruel twist of fate, Suranne developed the terrible disease. She had fought it hard with her husband Mick and their son by her side through chemotherapy and radiotherapy, but in the end the cancer had taken over her body. The chemo made her hair fall out and her immune system weak, and she became susceptible to illness and infection. Suranne wasn't getting any better and she, of all people, knew what the process would entail. She began requiring more help with simple day to day activities that many of us take for granted, such as washing and getting to the toilet on time. She became emotionally floored and eventually sat her son and husband down for a discussion that they'll never forget.

Suranne explained to them that she had spent her entire life caring for people, she bathed them when they couldn't do it themselves any longer, she changed their beds when they soiled themselves, she gave perfect strangers the most intimate and personal care another person could give. She remained with them in their dying days, in their last moments surrounded by their grieving families and had experienced more loss than anyone should have to. She had thought long and hard and had decided that, whilst she was still of sound mind and able to make her own decisions, she was going to plan her own death. She had told Mick that she didn't want to have to get to the point where he had to give her bed baths and wipe her arse for her. She wanted to die with her dignity intact. She explained to Mick and their son that this was her decision and she was going to take her own life when she felt the time was right. She explained to them that she was not going to tell them when or where or how, as she didn't want them having any part of it and risk being arrested for assisting her.

Obviously, Mick and her son were not happy with this decision at all but it was no longer their choice, Suranne had made them clear of her intentions and had explained the reasons why. After months of family deliberations, Mick and their son gave Suranne their blessing, knowing that she wouldn't do anything without it. They explained to me that as much as it hurt them every day to give their blessing, they knew it was what Suranne wanted and knew that by keeping her alive, she would be unhappy and become a shell of what she once was. Mick explained that he had left the house at 8am to go to work, their son left a short time later to attend a lecture at university.

When Mick arrived home from work early at 4pm, after ringing Suranne and receiving no answer, he found her in her bed lifeless. She had a large measuring jug on her bedside table, half filled with crushed tablets. Mick checked her pulse and Suranne felt cold to the touch. She wasn't breathing, and he knew his beautiful wife of 33 years had died peacefully by her own choice. He told me that his emotions were mixed and I could see the pain now etched on his face. He explained that he felt an unbearable pain in his chest of loss, but at the same time he felt complete relief. When I asked what he meant by relief, he explained that he had left the house every day at the same time to go to work, not knowing if his wife would be there to greet him when he returned home. He spends his work days preoccupied, worrying about her and ringing every hour or so to check that she was still with him. He explained that he was also filled with relief that Suranne was now at peace and no longer in pain. He explained that he rang the police and contacted an ambulance, and then their son Lee had arrived home. He explained shortly afterwards that I had arrived and the paramedics had not yet attended. Just as the words had left his mouth, the doorbell went and in came the paramedics.

We all went upstairs to Suranne's bedroom where the paramedics, using an ECG machine, pronounced Suranne as deceased. It was clear that she had died a few hours ago, as rigor mortis had set in and she was still and ice cold when I conducted the search of her body. It was my job then, to request Supervision and CID to attend the house and secure the scene. This was to make sure nothing was touched or moved until they arrived. The paramedics left, and once again I was left alone with Mick and Lee and Suranne upstairs. It was an uncomfortable wait for CID and Supervision, I felt like I was totally invading these people's personal space. They had just lost their wife and mother in the most heart-breaking manner and now they had a fresh faced newbie cop sat awkwardly in their kitchen, waiting for the circus to arrive. I wasn't allowed to let them move Suranne, or put her in a more comfortable position or tidy up, which they were asking to do. I felt awful for them.

It took well over an hour for everyone to arrive at the address. Due to it being suicide, a Detective Inspector, Coroner Liaison Officer, forensic scenes of crimes officer, CID, Sergeant and me, were all present. Everyone crammed into this small kitchen there were seven officers, Mick and Lee. That's seven different people bustling around their family home, searching, asking questions, seizing personal items, seizing medication and taking photographs of their lost loved one. Whilst all this was happening, Mick and Lee were being questioned to rule out any help or assistance from them which would amount to assisted suicide, which is still illegal in the UK and treated as a very serious offence.

I took a step back, surveyed the scene and felt totally gutted for these two men. At a time when they should have been allowed to grieve and pay their respects to Suranne, their house was filled with people, all with a different job to do, mostly losing sight that these two men had just had their world turned upside down. From this date, there have been many times within my policing career where it has saddened me to see cops of all ranks and length of service forget that we deal with people, real human beings with real feelings. The way they are dealt with could, and does, change the rest of their lives. Some cops just see them as another job, another bit of paperwork and in my opinion this is so wrong.

After this incident, I spent a long time in my career, volunteering for deaths and concern for welfare jobs. I felt confident that I could deal with them in a professional but empathetic manner. Most of the jobs I dealt with, I came away at the end of my shift feeling like I had done the best job I could, dealing with the deceased and their families professionally.

One job that will stay with me forever is a suicide I witnessed. I walked away that day an emotional mess, I blamed myself 100% for not finding this man quicker. This is what happened.

I was single crewed (that never changed, we were mostly out on our own) driving around in my fully-liveried police car, when the radio operator asked me to go to a job. I was asked to attend the local train station, where a member of the public had reported that an elderly gentleman had attempted to jump in front of a train. When I arrived, the train station was deserted, nobody at all was lingering about and nobody came up to me to let me know about the call. I honestly thought that it was a hoax, as we do receive many hoax calls to the police. Normally, I'd assume if you had seen somebody try and jump in front of a train and felt strongly enough to ring the police that surely you would stick around to give more details to the attending officer? They had not, and when the call taker re-contacted them, they said they had jumped on the next train as they had to get home. It all sounded a bit fishy. Despite this, there was a chance that it could be a genuine call so I double-checked the description with the radio operator. They relayed that the man was about 75 years old, he had short/shaved grey hair, he was carrying a walking stick and walked with a limp. The original caller also stated that this male had a hole in his neck, possibly from a tracheotomy operation.

The information I had been passed was quite specific so I started to think that this call may actually be genuine and as a result, I began to drive around the local area, looking out for someone that matched his description. He should have stuck out like a sore thumb but no matter where I looked I couldn't find him. It was like finding a needle in a hay stack and I was beginning to give up hope. After about fifty minutes of looking, I contacted the radio operator and told them that I had looked literally everywhere, but hadn't come across anyone matching this man's description.

It was rush hour and was really busy, with job after job coming in to the police. I was given a job on the other side of my division which meant I had to get on the motorway to get there. As I drove up the main road towards the slip road for the motorway, in front of me, in what seemed like slow motion, to my right hand side, I saw a figure leap head-first off the motorway bridge onto the motorway below. I heard tyres screeching and people screaming and I couldn't breathe, I felt sick. I knew this was my guy. The guy I should have found sooner. I sped up the road and blocked it with my cop car. I couldn't get out of it quick enough, I literally fell out of it onto the pavement. I ran over to the side of the bridge and looked over. What I witnessed is imprinted in my brain and I will never, ever forget what I saw. On the wrong side of the motorway bridge was the person's walking stick, wedged like a pole vault stick stuck up in the air. It had become wedged between the barrier and some metal light, overlooking the motorway. As I looked over, I could see the long tail-backs down the motorway. 40-50ft below, I saw a white transit van parked across two lanes of the motorway and behind it was the body of what I believed to be a man, on the inside lane of the motorway. You could see the man's brains strewn across all three lanes of the motorway, as the transit van had popped open his head like an orange. Then the smell of death hit me, I was confused, this man had only just died but already I could smell death? This was one of my worst experiences of my policing career. Without sounding disrespectful, this guy had just jumped off a bridge in front of me, and had been splattered by a transit van. What other job would you have to deal with something so horrific, but then have to put on a brave face and take charge? This is exactly what I did, there was nobody else there to do it, so I had to. I was so angry with the public, crowds were gathering on the bridge and the surrounding streets, all trying to look over the barriers at the guy on the motorway. I had already radioed through to update everybody. It turned out that another local policing unit was already on the motorway, stuck in the tail-backs heading towards the man. Using the hard shoulder, they made their way slowly towards him. I started to shift the crowds, then attempted to direct the officers to shut off certain roads and tape off the scene on top of the bridge. I was constantly updating the supervision by my radio, and I heard that the officers on the motorway had been asked if they could check if the man had the tracheostomy scar because if he didn't, then we would have to resume the search for the original male. It was obvious that it was the same guy, but they had to check. I then heard the update that the officers couldn't actually tell, because the man's head and neck was in such a bad way. As a result, and now other officers had arrived to preserve my scene, I was asked to continue looking for the original male until paramedics confirmed this man's identity. I got back in my police car and drove away from the scene, about one hundred metres away in fact, before I had to pull the car over. Emotions of every type filled my body and I lost control of them. I totally broke down, I was struggling to breathe and hot, salty tears ran down my face. I felt like a fool, passers-by looking at me like I had two heads. Police officers aren't meant to show emotion, they are supposed to be strong, supposed to maintain self-control and here I was sat in a police car, unbeknown to any of my colleagues, a shaking, crying mess. I was full-on sobbing when a kind lady knocked on my window and asked if I was ok, if she could help me in any way. Barely able to talk I thanked her and I explained that I would be fine. Back on my own, I couldn't stop thinking that I had failed this man in the worst possible way. I hadn't found him in time, maybe if I had driven up this road a little sooner, maybe I would have been able to convince him that life was worth living? Maybe if I hadn't pulled over to write down the details of the next job, I may have found him sooner? I felt like his death was on my head. I felt like I had failed as a police officer, and as a person. Sat alone on the side of the road I knew I was in no fit state to drive, but felt embarrassed and ashamed at my lack of self-control and my emotional state, so didn't want to contact my supervisor. I decided to ring my partner, who is also a cop, and I knew that he would understand everything I was going through without judgement. He always knew what to say to me, to make me see sense and make me calm down. After a good twenty minutes' chat with him, I calmed down. As I hadn't responded to my radio in a while, my Sergeant 'point to pointed' me, this means he made a personal call to my radio. I explained that I was a little upset and blamed myself for this man's death, and that I was not in a fit state to drive. He attended my location to collect me and the drive back to the police station felt like the drive of shame, in silence. Everyone now knew I had broken down, and had to be collected by the Sergeant, I felt totally embarrassed.

Showing weakness in the police is not the done thing. If you do, it's guaranteed that you are the talk of the station and the odd one out. I was told by my Sergeant that I should go home, but I wasn't allowed to drive home by myself. My kids were in bed asleep so my partner couldn't come, so I started to ring around the people I knew would be finished at work. After the seventh phone call, someone finally answered and agreed to come and collect me. I felt useless. Whilst waiting for my lift, my Inspector arrived at the police station. When she came into the office, she said, "Oh, you're a sensitive soul aren't you?" I felt like screaming at her, I already felt like shit, felt embarrassed and I just wanted to shout at her, tell her that I had just seen a man jump off a bridge and fall to his death, seen his head squashed on the road, his brains strewn across three lanes of the motorway. I felt like it was my fault, like I should have been able to save him. And I'm sensitive? But that's the cops for you, you show weakness and you're the odd one out, the weak link.

After the event, I found out that this guy had just left the hospital after being given only three months to live. He had had cancer several times in his life, but this time his body couldn't fight it. He had then decided to take his own life, rather than wait for the inevitable. I began to realise that even if I had gotten to him, if I had got there in time on that day, he would have tried again and again and again, until he succeeded. I no longer blamed myself, with hindsight in my favour. I felt angry with him though, for being so bloody selfish. He did this in rush hour, in front of hundreds of members of the public. There were men, women and children in the cars on the motorway. The guy who was driving the van that hit him will have that horrific day etched in his mind for ever. I feel sad for this man to think that he had nothing left, so he had to take his own life. How much guts it must have taken to do what he did. I just feel sad for him and despite never knowing him, I will never forget him.

Although the next job I am about to describe ended a little differently than the ones before, I wanted to include it in this section because this lady will also stay with me forever, and for her I do believe that I did everything possible. I do believe that the actions of another officer and his arrogant, narcissistic ways caused this job to go completely tits up.

A job came in to the police from a man who worked at the local train station. He said that there was a lady on a bridge, threatening to jump off. I was literally around the corner and was at the train station in a matter of seconds. It was about 8 o'clock at night and would have been pitch black, if it wasn't for the platform lights. I sprinted up the platform and found the railway worker who had contacted us. He was pointing towards the end of the platform, which was in total darkness. As I approached, I saw a dark figure sat on the wall across the tracks from me.

There were two sets of live train tracks in front of me and a lady threatening to jump. I had no idea how high the drop on the other side was, or even what she would drop onto, as I wasn't familiar with this area. I was torn, my instinct was to go over to her and try and talk her down, but I knew that the tracks were live and a train could speed through the station at any time. I started talking to her. I asked her name, but she just told me to "FUCK OFF". She was visibly upset and crying. I radioed through and updated everyone, and asked them to put the trains on the lines on hold urgently. I knew I would get an arse-kicking if I even attempted to get on the tracks without confirmation that the trains had been stopped. I carried on talking to her, telling her who I was and explaining that I could help her. I saw her look down the platform to my right in panic. She started to stand up on the wall and my heart began to race. I shouted to all the cops that were running towards me to back off. I gave a clear update on the radio that nobody was to approach us, as it was making the female panicky and she was teetering on the edge. I stated clearly on the radio several times that the lady had told me that if anyone else tried to approach us, she would definitely jump and I genuinely believed her.

I must have said this over and over about seven times but still officers attempted to get closer, sneaking behind the train shelters and the advertisement boards. The woman could see their shadows, so stood up and shakily climbed to a higher point of the wall, which was another five feet up. I panicked and once again told them to back off and reiterated on the radio that nobody was to approach. I was having to maintain contact with this lady, building up a rapport so she trusted me, and also having to make sure no other cop took it upon themselves to come on over and try to be a hero. I was then told that a complete stop had been put on the lines so it was safe for me to get closer to her. As I walked over the tracks, I saw that the wall in front of me was about five feet high, the part where she was stood was ten feet high. I stood with rocks under foot and looked over the other side of the wall, where she was currently standing the drop was about sixty feet. I saw that if she came back down to the lower part of the wall, the drop would be about thirty feet on to a corrugated garage workshop roof.

I updated everyone and started to talk to her, we spoke for what felt like an age, but I bet it was really only about ten or fifteen minutes. She told me that she had been badly physically, sexually and mentally abused as a child and teenager. She told me that she had been through years of therapy and had even summoned the courage to stand up in court against her abuser, sending him to prison. The reason she felt so low was that earlier on that day she had received a phone call from someone official, telling her that her abuser was being released five years early. She explained that she felt devastated and felt like the criminal justice system had badly let her down. She looked like a broken woman and I felt helpless for her as I didn't know what I could do to help her.

I posed the question, "What could I do for you right now that would make you feel a little better?"

She replied, "Get me a cig and a lighter."

She looked pretty desperate and, still building up the rapport, I felt like I could use this to make the situation a little safer. I struck a deal with her. I would facilitate her request if she kindly got down from the very high wall she was on, and came down to the lower wall she was on before. She took ages mulling over the deal but finally agreed, on the one condition that nobody came close to her, or she would jump. She climbed down and at one point, my heart was in my mouth as she almost slipped and fell over the wrong side of the wall. Once she was down, she shuffled up the wall a bit, to where she had left her handbag. I hadn't seen this before as I was concentrating on her, and it was dark. I placed my arm across the wall, knowing that she wouldn't come back this way to the high bit, through fear of me pulling her down. I radioed through my request for the cigarette and lighter, and specifically stated that nobody was to approach us and that when it was safe to do so, they should throw it over to me in a bag. I could hear other officers on the radio, contacting ambulances and the fire brigade in case she fell, and to open the big, metal gates that lead into the car yard below. I could see in the distance, the lights of the police cars cordoning off the roads and attempting to move the curious onlookers. I could hear that a professional negotiator had been contacted and that there was quite a delay in getting to us. I also saw that trains had started to pull into the station on the other platform and worried that the stop hadn't actually been placed on the line after all. I was praying that no trains came towards me. The officer with the lighter was taking ages and the lady was becoming agitated as she had stuck to her part of the deal and she just wanted a cigarette. It was beginning to look to her like I was misleading her. I radioed through again within ear-shot of the lady, and specifically requested that a person met me half way, and specifically not to approach us, as I didn't want the lady to jump. I received no reply. I was desperately trying to keep this lady calm. I went to take hold of her hand to calm her down and comfort her, she flinched, but when I explained that it was merely to offer her comfort and I promised I wouldn't attempt to pull her down, she allowed me to take her hand. If I had attempted to pull her down at this point, she would have fallen over and taken me with her, so it wasn't an option for me.

I now knew that I had earned her trust and I was getting somewhere with talking to her, and making her realise that this wasn't the way to deal with this situation. Whilst we were deep in conversation I heard footsteps on the platform behind me, my heart sank and I turned to see my Inspector standing there. He had brought the lady a cigarette and lighter, but had completely disregarded my constant request to remain alone with this lady. She took one look at him, let go of my hand and went to stand up. She began shouting at me, "YOU LIED TO ME, YOU LIED TO ME!" She told me that I was just like all the others and she couldn't trust anybody. I pleaded with her and tried to explain that I didn't know that he was coming, that I had kept my word and he had come over all by himself without telling me. She was having none of it, all the rapport I had built, all the trust I had earned had vanished. Thinking fast on my feet and not wanting her to jump, I went and took the lit cigarette off my Inspector and offered it to her if she sat down. She took it, walked away turning her back to me, out of my reach and sat down smoking it. At this point I would have tried anything to stop her from jumping off this bridge, so I gestured to the Inspector that I was considering trying to pull her backwards, off the bridge towards me to try and save her. He took one look at me and, shaking his head mouthed, "DON'T YOU DARE". I was torn, did I try it and risk disobeying an order, with the added risk of her falling anyway, or did I leave her and do as I was told, hoping and praying that she wouldn't jump.

A split second later, with the cigarette in her mouth, she dangled herself over the edge and jumped. I heard her hit the corrugated roof and scream. I climbed up on the wall, sat down and shouted over to her, asking if she was ok. Silly really, but I just wanted her to answer me, make a noise or something? She had fallen thirty feet landing on corrugated metal. Finally, she began to cry out in pain and I felt relief. I turned to the Inspector and reiterated that I had told him not to come over, as I was dealing with the situation. I started talking to the lady and I could see that the ambulance and the fire brigade were struggling to get through the huge, metal gates that secured the yard which she had fallen into. When they eventually gained entry, they had the obstacle of getting onto the garage roof, which was about ten feet high from the floor where they were standing. It probably wasn't the safest roof to be clambering on either. I watched all the people below, like busy ants trying to formulate their plan of how to get to the lady. All the while I kept talking to her, reassuring her that help would be with her very soon. Once the paramedic first responder got to her, I stopped shouting down reassurance and got down off the wall as she was in safe hands now.

As I climbed back onto the safety of the platform, a train came along the track minutes later, a British transport officer told me that there had been a miscommunication between forces, and no 'stop' had actually been placed on the lines which I had been standing on. I must have had someone looking over me that night, keeping me safe. I was so angry though, firstly with my Inspector, who completely disregarded my request for him and others to stay away from us. In my opinion if he hadn't come over, eventually I would have been able to talk her down. Secondly, with the utter incompetence of people who could have cost me my life by telling me that there was a 'stop' placed on the line.

Catching my breath and gaining professional composure, I walked down to the yard where a meeting was taking place between the fire commander and the paramedic commander. I approached them, giving them all the information I could, then made my way into the yard. A huge operation was under way, the fire brigade had a large crane attached to their specialised fire engine. On top of this was a platform with a few specialist medics who were trained to work at height. Eventually, after about an hour, they got her down on a spinal board and went off as safely as possible to hospital. There was a multi-agency debrief in the yard straight after which I should have really attended, but my Inspector told me I had to go back to the police station for our own debrief. I guess that this was so I didn't drop him in it and tell everyone that he shouldn't have come over to us, and that I had given a serious request that nobody was to approach us.

Anyhow, I went back to the police station as requested. I was still seething with him; I didn't want to speak to him, let alone be in the same room debriefing one major fuck up by him. In my opinion, if he had actually listened to me for once in his life, rather than let his rank go to his head thinking that he knew better, then maybe I would have been able to talk this lady down and she would have been ok and uninjured.

I did as I was told and attended the debrief with several other officers. The Inspector went through the forty plus page log line by line, asking everybody to explain their role and to justify all their actions, whilst he wrote the notes down in his daybook. We got to each line where I had specifically asked for people to stay back and not approach, as the lady was threatening to jump if they did. Line after line were written; my requests for people to stay away, not to approach. I hadn't the self-control any longer to keep quiet and bite my tongue. My words came spilling out like verbal poop.

"Why do you always think you know better just because you're an Inspector?"

"I've been doing the job for ten years, why could you not trust my judgement call?"

"What exactly were you thinking?"

His answer was simple, and made my blood boil,

"Good practice and normal protocol in this situation, is that you have two officers within ear shot of the person at all times, to cover the first officer's back. This is so nobody thinks you are saying anything bad to the person on the bridge like 'jump', for example."

I could have flipped my lid there and then in that cramped office filled with officers. I felt like screaming in the Inspector's face or actually walloping him! It took an immense amount of self-control not to do either. As an acting Inspector, they are renowned for sticking to policy and protocol to the letter, trying to do everything by the book. I do understand that in most circumstances, this works and provides a professional service to the public; however, this is real life. Things, situations and real-life people do not fit into boxes outlined in a text book. Sometimes, certain situations call for policies and protocols to be thrown out of the window and used as a guidance only whilst actually dealing with the job using common sense.

It genuinely pisses me off when you get a total jobs worth, who think they know better because they are a higher rank. They seem to forget that they are police officers too and did the same job as us not that long ago. They forget that they are human beings and are also susceptible to making mistakes, sometimes big ones. It has become apparent though, that in the police, the higher up the ranks you climb, the easier it is to "justify" your decisions and actions and because you are of high rank, little or no questions are asked.

I can't believe I was still sat in this debrief, but we got to the part where the woman was on the bridge, and the Inspector told me I wasn't to try and pull her back to save her. I told him that I thought he was totally wrong to tell me not to do this, and in hindsight, I don't believe that this amounted to a lawful order. I explained that, at the time, I was seriously considering ignoring him and trying to save her anyway. He said, if I had disobeyed a "lawful order", then I would have been in serious trouble. He explained that the reason he gave that order was because in training, they are told never to take hold of anyone in case they jump and it looked like you had pushed them, or in case they pulled you over with them. I again lost my temper. I told him that in hindsight, I didn't believe that it was a genuine lawful order, how could he order me not to try and save someone's life? I explained that in the position which I was in looking up at the lady five feet above me, there was no chance that she could have pulled me over, but if I had been allowed the chance to try and save her I may well have done.

I've been informed since that the lady didn't die from her injuries, but will be in a wheelchair for the rest of her life, unable to walk or possibly care for herself at all. She has suffered a broken pelvis, broken her spine in several places and suffered a broken leg and arm. To this day, I do regret not trying to save her. I regret not trying to pull her down, but I no longer feel responsible for the final outcome. I feel that this responsibility lies completely and wholly with the Inspector on the day. He was so full of himself that he lacked any common sense or management skills.

MURDER

I have attended as the 'first responder' to quite a few murders and attempted murders. Two of the jobs that I remember clearly are explained next. These are the jobs that I can picture as if it was yesterday, people's actions, what I saw, what I smelled, what I said, what they said, all etched in my memory.

The first job was horrific; I was sat taking a statement from a burglary victim in their house. It was about 9am and the police radio was generally quiet for a Tuesday morning. I heard the radio spring to life with a report from the ambulance service of having found a young woman at home, tied to her bed, with various injuries. I was listening intently to the updates that kept on coming from the radio operator. The first update was that the female was alive and breathing but unconscious. The next update was that the paramedics at the scene had declared the lady's life extinct, she had died. Due to being short-staffed, I had already made my apologies to the burglary victim I was sat with, and was in my police van on my way to the house. I was approximately fifteen minutes away whilst travelling at normal road speed. I heard that a single-crewed officer had arrived at the address. I was concentrating on driving and listening intently to the updates. The officer was calm when he began to update the radio operator on the situation he had attended. He explained that the lady was about twenty four years old and lived at home with her two young children. The kids were nine months old and three years old. The kids' dad was still in an on/off relationship with the lady, and stayed at the address a lot. The lady usually contacts her mother-in-law on a Tuesday morning, as she assists in the childcare of the two little ones to give her a break. Today, the mother-in-law had received no contact from the lady, so she went around to the house to check on her and the kids. On her arrival, she found the front door unlocked and the back door wide open. The three-year-old was locked, crying in the living room. She went to look for her daughter-in-law and other, younger grandchild. She walked into the main bedroom and found them both in the most horrific scene. Her daughter-in-law was tied to her bed, with multiple injuries, soaked in blood. She didn't know if she was dead or alive, as the blood was coming from multiple places, and she couldn't bring herself to get too close to her. The poor baby was on the bed with its mother, thankfully uninjured, but also covered in its mother's blood, its nappy full with soaked-up blood.

The mother-in-law, grabbing the baby frantically, contacted the ambulance and then rang for her husband to come to the address. She carried the baby downstairs to the living room, where the other child sat inconsolable. She sat there feeling numb, trying to absorb what she had just encountered. The paramedics arrived and declared that the lady had died. Her father-in-law, en route to the address, had contacted the lady's family. He arrived at the house with the first police officer.

Listening to the officer on the radio, he explained that he currently had the murder scene upstairs and in the living room the two paramedics, the two children and the mother - and father-in-law of the deceased lady.

Suddenly I heard the panic in the officer's voice and then he pressed his emergency button, so you could hear everything in the background. The officer was telling somebody to back off and then tried to tell the radio operator that five members of the deceased's family had arrived at the address and were physically trying to force their way in to see their loved one. The officer was on his own, trying to tell them that he had to keep the scene secure.

I, along with every other officer who had heard the commotion, used their emergency equipment on their cars and rushed to assist. We pretty much all arrived at the same time and managed to calm the situation down. Understandably, her family were very upset, so in the most diplomatic way possible, we assisted the original officer to secure the scene.

A short time later, CID and supervision arrived at the house. They took over the investigation with the assistance of specialised forensic officers. This was whilst uniformed officers like myself, stayed in static points around the address, securing the scene for twenty four hours. I did three shifts of duty on the scene over a period of three days, and watched as passers-by tried to have a nosey. Reporters came and went, news crews came, filmed then left, knocking at neighbours for any information they could gather. Stood there in my hi-vis and hat for eight hours at a time was exhausting, especially as the weather was so bad and I got drenched daily, but it was totally worth it.

Eventually, the whole truth emerged. The lady and her children's father had been in a physically violent relationship that was constantly ending, then starting up again. The lady had never reported any violence to the police, but had had enough of it all and was planning on leaving him, and the area, and taking their children with her. She was planning on moving them all to the other side of the country. She had summoned up the courage that morning to tell her fella, via text message, that the relationship was over. He then, in response, hurried around to her house and let himself in. He confronted her and they had a heated argument. He had hold of the three-year-old, so she took the baby upstairs to get out of the way. He followed her soon after, locking the toddler in the living room. The argument continued and she let slip that she was moving away. The male saw red and in a blind rage began to physically punch the lady about her head, causing her to eventually lose consciousness. Whilst she was unconscious, he tied her to the bed and raped her whilst the baby looked on. She came around and began to tell him he was a bully and a monster. He stormed out of the bedroom, and down the stairs, into the back garden. Here, he retrieved an uprooted paving slab which he carried back up the stairs and back into the bedroom. He began to smash the slab into her head and body, a blind rage fuelling his actions, he raped her again and again. Blood everywhere, he continued to beat her and rape her. Once her heart had stopped beating and her last breath had left her body, he raped her corpse one last time before leaving his baby on the bed, soaked in its mother's blood. He left his three-year-old in the living room and got in his car, driving off. He made no attempt to raise any help for his partner or his children. He just drove and drove and after the lady was found in the state that she was in, a marker was placed on his car. He was stopped by traffic officers on the other side of the country the next day. I know that he will now be spending a very long time in prison for his crimes. I feel sorry for their children; I hope that they never find out what their mother truly went through, or what a controlling monster their father is.

The second serious job I remember so clearly was on a Friday night, late in December. I was in company with another bobby who was chauffeuring me around the division in a clapped-out old panda. We had a few officers ring in sick that evening, so we were short-staffed until the overlap shift came on at 9pm. That generally isn't a problem, as it stays quiet before 9pm on a Friday night. So, in all, there were about four cars driving about the division on patrol. Our beat was Sunny Bridge and we got a report of a domestic incident ongoing. The radio operator told us that a neighbour, who was still on the phone to the call taker, had rung, concerned for the safety of a lady across the road. She explained that a man and lady had just walked up her street, screaming at one another. As they went into number 10, the man hit the lady in her face so hard, it caused her to stumble and fall into the door.

With this information in hand, the job just became a whole lot more urgent and my colleague used his emergency equipment on the car to make our way faster. Jobs like these unnerve me, not knowing what you are going to, not knowing who you are going to be dealing with, how big they are, what background they have, if there are any dogs in the house, any weapons in the house, any other people?

Your adrenaline starts to pump through your veins, you go quiet and start to concentrate on what eventualities you may be faced with. As we neared the address, we received the update that the male had started to punch the lady about her face and body. We were nearly there, it felt like time was standing still and we couldn't get there fast enough. My heart was in my throat, hoping and praying that she was ok. Hoping that we could help her. The next update took my breath away and sent shivers and goose bumps around my body. HE HAD A KNIFE, HE WAS STABBING HER REPEATEDLY! The radio operator relayed the information to us and when we arrived, I realised I was still sat there holding my breath.

With no second thought that there may be a knife-wielding mad man nearby I practically fell out of the police car. I stood on the pavement and in a nanosecond, surveyed the scene in front of me. There were people everywhere, a lady was lying half in and half out of the threshold of the door. I could hear her gurgling; I've heard that sound before when a man punctured his lung from a stab wound. There was blood everywhere, on the floor, smeared up the walls, the lady was covered in it. Another lady was knelt beside her, putting pressure on as many of her wounds as she could. She identified herself as one of her neighbours but also an A and E nurse at the local hospital. She stated that she had called for an ambulance and I asked if there was anything I could do to assist her. She explained that she had pretty much got it under control and any further people or hands would just complicate things. It would have been daft for me to try and take over when this lady had medical training and was doing an amazing job, so I left her to it with the intention of securing the scene, clearing the crowd and gathering potential witnesses. I was updating the radio operator with the scene when I heard a shout, "HE'S JUST RUN DOWN THERE!"

I saw my colleague set off running in the direction that the bloke pointed in. I was torn, I didn't know if I should stay with the lady or go and help Dom, my colleague. In a split second, I realised that the lady was in good hands and the scene outside had already been compromised by the onlookers, so I made off after Dom. We didn't know if this offender still had the knife, we didn't know how big or violent he was, so I ran as fast as I could. I caught Dom up, overtook him and found the guy hot-footing it down the main road towards the town centre. I was so intent on getting to the male offender, that I didn't see a young lad run past me. He went to punch the guy square in the face, but Dom managed to get to him in a split second and stopped him. Dom and this young lad, who turned out to be the victim's son, were tussling on the floor, as the lad was so upset and worked up about seeing his mother in such a state. I grabbed the offender, I shoved him in handcuffs and sat him on the floor. He didn't put up much of a fight but he was much bigger than I was and I wasn't sure if he still had possession of the knife. I searched him as best as I could whilst he was sat down, to avoid any injury to myself.

I updated the radio operator that I had arrested the male and was comfortable dealing with him on my own until Dom had calmed the son down. I directed the first patrols that passed me, straight to the scene. Now secure in handcuffs, I surveyed the man in front of me, and he was definitely not what I had pictured on the drive up to the address. He was older, maybe in his fifties, he was of rotund build, about 5ft 6 with grey hair and glasses. He was wearing some sort of corduroy trousers and a shirt. He kind of reminded me of my dad. That is, apart from the congealed blood he had all over his hands and clothes. There were big bits of skin and blood clots all over him, which I assumed were from the injured lady. He had blood, snot and tears all over his face and he was sat on the floor sobbing.

I was aware that officers and paramedics were now with the injured lady, so I told him that he was under arrest for attempted murder. He was shocked, and asked why he was being arrested for attempted murder? He said that he intended to kill her, why isn't she dead?

I asked for a police van to transport him to the custody office. Whilst we sat there, it obviously registered with him, that the lady was still alive and he started to repeat over and over,

"This is my confession, you best write it down miss, because this is the only time I'm going to say it."

I got out my pocket note book and began to write. He continued to speak and said words to the effect of,

"I fully meant to kill the fucking bitch. I fucking hate her, I hope that she's dead. I stabbed her, then I couldn't stop stabbing her, I've had enough."

I wrote down his words, exactly as he said them. The van arrived and I followed him to the police custody office. Here, I booked him in with the custody Sergeant. I read his confession back to him whilst he was being visually and audibly recorded in the presence of the custody Sergeant. I then gave him the opportunity to agree to what I had written, and sign it if he believed that they were the true words he had said. He took that opportunity to sign it, and began to repeat that he hoped she died.

I found out a few shifts later that the man had worked for many years at a local hospital as a senior mental health nurse, on the psychiatric wards. His victim, and partner, was a nurse on the same ward. It turned out that he had stabbed her approximately 27 times, in various parts of her body. Amazingly and thankfully, the lady survived. I believe that she suffered a punctured lung, punctured liver and punctured kidney. She was very poorly and very lucky to be alive. The offender eventually went to court, and pleaded guilty at his first hearing to Attempted Murder, meaning that there was no trial, and his victim didn't have to attend court. He was sentenced to eleven years in prison.

This happened approximately eight years ago, which means that the offender is probably out of prison by now. The victim will have to live with the emotional and physical effects for the rest of her life. Her children, who are adults, will always have those images of seeing their mother practically dying in front of them. The poor neighbour who stepped up as the nurse on the night, and literally saved the lady's life, and every police officer who attended and witnessed the devastating scene, will have it etched in their memories forever. It's been eight years and I can still remember every graphic detail. Every smell, every word spoken. A real caring copper never forgets victims like that, they just try and bury it in a place in their mind, to allow room for the next job and victim.

PERSONAL LOSS

In this section, it is going to be difficult not to mention certain officers' names. Out of respect for those officers, and their families, I believe that it is appropriate to name them. Most names and times in this section are fact, not changed or made up; the dates may vary due to poor memory.

When I started my policing career as a Special Constable, I was almost nineteen years old. As a regular officer, I was twenty years old, and had dealt with death at work. I had never, however, lost anybody close to me. I thought that if it happened, I would be fine, that it would just be like dealing with the death of a stranger at work. Oh, how wrong was I?

My first experience of personal loss was after being in the cops for about four years. I had just returned from maternity leave, and was posted at a new station, in a new area, with a new team of cops to get to know and work with. I found my place within the team, but due to only working 75% hours, I always felt like the outsider, but that's another chapter.

Anyhow, a few officers made me feel welcome, Ian Rowley was one of them. He was forty eight years old, which was older than my dad at the time, but in his head, he was still in his twenties. He had been in the police for a very long time, and was one of the good cops, respected by colleagues and the community alike.

He was an old-school beat bobby, who lived where he worked. It seemed to me that he knew practically everyone by name, and they all knew him. He changed the opinion of a lot of the community on the police, for the better, and helped raise money for the Help the Heroe's charity with one of the local residents, who otherwise would have probably ended up in prison. This is where Ian and I clicked, I loved raising money for charity, and offered to help him in my spare time. He was a quirky individual. You certainly knew when Ian had entered the building. He would poke a Lycra-clad leg around the door frame, singing to the ladies. He cycled to and from work in his full Lycra cycling pants and top. These, in my opinion, were far too tight in the groin area, and we always had a laugh, I would tell him to stop shoving socks down his trollies and in response, he'd raise his leg up on the chair and do his lunges, all done whilst sporting his 1970s porn tash. Most of all, I can remember Ian being a generous, happy, caring man. If you needed help, it was never too much effort for him. He was kind and trustworthy, and helped me to fit into both the team, and the local community.

One day, whilst off duty, I was at home with my daughter, when I received a phone call from my supervisor. He told me that Ian had died. It was his 49th birthday, he had felt poorly in the night and had slept in the spare room. His wife had said goodbye before leaving for work in the morning, then on her return, she had found Ian and he had sadly died.

His funeral was the first I had ever been to. I didn't know what to expect, but I did know that Ian was proud to be a police officer, so I knew I had to wear my best uniform. I put on my tunic, best trousers and super-shiny boots. I arrived at work early in the morning on the day of his funeral. I had spent hours the previous evening, trying to shine and 'bull' my boots. I was proud of their slight shine, but two of my colleagues, who were ex-army, demanded I removed my boots. Within ten minutes, you could see your face in the toes of my boots. I knew Ian would be happy with us.

Walking up to the small, local church, I felt weird. I had only been laughing with him the week before, and now the pall bearers carried him in his cold, dark coffin, with his tall police hat balancing on top. It was so emotional, I could not hold back the tears. It felt so totally wrong, he was far too young to die, he was a good person, why him? Then again, I'm sure everybody feels the same way about their friends or loved ones. Rest in peace Ian Rowley, you are gone but never forgotten, the force lost one of its best that day.

The next time I experienced a personal loss was a day that the whole country will remember, September 18th 2012. I was on maternity leave with my second child. We were shopping in town, and I was trying on clothes in River Island, getting extremely upset that nothing would fit. My son, asleep in his trolley, and my partner, sat outside waiting for me to try on the hundredth item. He was also a cop, on the same division as me. We were both aware that a dirty cretin was on the run, for the murders of two people in Droylsden. Single-crewed unarmed officers were not allowed to go anywhere near him, or any addresses linked to him, directly or indirectly. My partner received a text message whilst I was in the changing room, still stropping about clothes. I heard his voice break when he asked me to come out and speak to him. He told me that the low life cretin had finally been captured. I smiled a massive smile and sighed a sigh of relief, saying out loud, "Thank God". My partner didn't look pleased at all; the colour had drained from his face. He said that two officers had been shot. We were being updated by a friend and colleague and the information was completely confidential, so we couldn't check on the news or anything. I immediately assumed that it would be two firearms officers that had attended, given who they had located, and thought their injuries wouldn't be life-threatening, due to their ballistic protection.

We were updated again. It wasn't firearms officers, it was two response female officers from our station; unarmed and unaware of what they were on their way to face, responding to a normal burglary call.

Still being updated, we were told that PC Fiona Bone had been killed instantly at the scene; however, PC Nicola Hughes was still alive and on her way to the hospital.

Time stood still. I couldn't breathe. I couldn't function. We left everything where it was in the shop, and left to get in the car. Both my partner and I held it together until we got in the car. We placed our small, sleeping son in his car seat, grateful of his deep slumber. We both sat there in silence. Silent, salty tears running down our faces. I had no words. I had slight hope that Nick would pull through, praying that she would be ok. We only had the information that we had been told and were clinging to our phones for news, any news. Soon, still sat in that empty, desolate car park, we received the news that Nick had also died. That's when the sobs came, and wouldn't pass. We both just sat frozen, unable to move.

I had only been out with Fiona the week before and the rest of the shift at another officer's leaving party. We sat in the Comedy Store chuckling at the comics, then went to the club next door. I'm not much of a dancer, so stayed sat down and chatted to Fiona about her soon-to-be-wife Claire, and her step daughter, who she told me she adored. We talked about meeting up with the kids at a play area and treating them, one day soon. She was full of joy for the future, her wedding was imminent and her life was to be complete. A wave of sadness washed over me again. I felt so sad for her fiancé Claire, and her daughter Jessie. If I felt the way I did, I couldn't even begin to imagine how they were feeling.

Due to my maternity leave, I hadn't had the pleasure of getting to know Nicola. Whenever I passed her in the corridor, she would always light the place up with her massive smile. I often heard her making people laugh, and at twenty three years old, she was beautiful, bright and had the rest of her life ahead of her. My partner knew Nicola well and thought very highly of her. Even now, he talks about her with a smile, whilst remembering this little lady who had the power to light up a room with her smile.

We managed to get home through the tears and emotion. Once home, we switched on the television and there were our girls faces, strewn across the media. Gobsmacked, we thought that there may be some media coverage, but how the hell had they found out the officers' identities? My heart sank, I hoped and prayed that their families had been told first. I hoped that they hadn't had to find out from the news.

It turned out that the police service had some officers and civilian staff who will do anything for money. It became common knowledge afterwards, that the media had an inside informant. We just hoped that eventually they would find out. One of the staff in the control room faced criminal and internal investigations for doing just this.

Following this awful day, it also became public knowledge that an actual police officer was passing information to the offender's family about the policing operation, which was in place in an attempt to capture him for the two previous murders. The information she passed allowed the scumbag to evade the police long enough to plan his horrific finale. The deaths of both ladies lay heavily on the shoulders of that officer who was, thankfully, convicted and sent to prison for her crimes. I, along with other colleagues, will never forgive her for her actions.

The day of the girls' funerals was coming up, and the support shown to us by the rest of the country was breath-taking. An officer had set up a Facebook site, rallying the support of officers, up and down the country. Hundreds and thousands of officers were offering their support. They were offering to come and spend a shift in our area and work for free, to enable every GMP officer who wanted to attend the girls' funerals. It was amazing how total strangers had become united by a common purpose, and by an occupation that puts them in danger every day. I was still on maternity leave, so was distanced from any plans about getting the division covered.

My partner and I went up to the scene in Hattersley to lay flowers. He was in uniform, I was not. We had our son in his car seat, as we couldn't get childcare. All we wanted to do is lay flowers and pay our respects, but I felt suffocated by journalists. They seemed to be trying to get pictures of us with our son in his seat. I made my fella take off his coat and cover our son. I just wanted to lay flowers in peace, that was a hard day.

I was invited to take part in a vigil that was being held

up in Hattersley, at the end of Abbey Gardens. Myself and approximately forty colleagues wore our full, smart uniforms and walked from Hyde police station, two by two, along the main roads up to Hattersley. Once we arrived, we stood side by side, shoulder to shoulder with the residents who had all turned out en masse, to show their respects to our girls. There were hundreds of people, who, like the officers, friends, families and colleagues, felt the loss of these two beautiful ladies.

The weather was not on our side and it didn't just rain, the heavens opened and it poured. This didn't put anybody off, officers stood to attention, raindrops mixing with tears running down their faces, rain filling the rims of our hats, residents stood, hoods up and a mass of umbrellas. The families of Nicola and Fiona attended, as did some very senior officers and the Chief Constable of Greater Manchester Police, Sir Peter Fahy. It felt like rank went out of the window that day, we were all equal, all humans, all grieving. For some officers, standing to attention under those circumstances proved too much. One officer collapsed. I was stood next to him and heard his hat hit the floor. With news cameras everywhere, I knew the officer would be being looked after by the officers behind us, so me and another colleague, John, stepped together to shield the officer from any news crews or cameras.

I didn't know how I was still standing emotionally, I had nothing left, but seeing people attend to lay flowers kept me stood there to attention. Up came the local fire brigade, paramedics, nurses, doctors and when they had paid their respects, it was our turn. Once we paid our respects, we walked side by side, back to Hyde police station. We arrived back, dripping wet through, emotionally and physically drained and exhausted. I went straight home and slept for as long as I could.

The day of Nicola's funeral arrived Wednesday 3rd October 2012, a day that touched the entire country. Both my partner and I got up extra early. The children were with family, we were dressed in our best uniform. We arrived at Ashton police station to take our places on the coaches provided for us by GMP.

The mood was low, the coaches almost silent, barely a whisper could be heard. Every officer was wearing their best uniform; some had only ever worn it once before, when they were sworn in as a police constable. As we got into the city centre I started to become emotional, the eyes of the world were on these funerals. We, as the police force, had received well wishes from as far away as America and Australia. As we pulled along the roads leading to Manchester Cathedral, I was totally speechless. Thousands of officers stood in full uniform, lining the streets. They stood shoulder to shoulder, rank and file and saluted as we passed. Officers from pretty much every police force in England, Wales and Scotland had attended in full uniform, to line our route and the route of Nicola and her family. It was said that officers had flown in from as far as Australia to be part of this day for the girls. Behind these saluting officers there were thousands and thousands of everyday people bowing their heads in respect as we passed. If any person reading this book attended on either of these days, I just want to thank you from the bottom of my heart. The country came together, united in one cause to lay a beautiful lady to rest.

We arrived and we were shown to our seats inside the cathedral. I was aware that the service was being broadcast on large screens outside, but whilst you sat there you forgot. The cathedral felt so small as Nicola was carried in, her bowler hat balancing on top of her small coffin. I broke. I could no longer stand. My legs gave way, how could she be gone? How could she be in that box and only twenty three years old? Devastated doesn't even go a little way towards explaining how I felt. When the lady Iona Fisher began to sing, every emotion you could ever feel washed over me. I felt anger and hate towards that evil cretin that took her away. I felt pain and anguish that this was final and felt upset, weak and vulnerable at showing so much raw emotion whilst in the presence of so many others. When we left to get back on the coaches, you could see that the crowds had brought the whole of Manchester City centre to a standstill. Thousands of people there just to show unity and pay their respects. It was extraordinary and a scene that will always stay imprinted on my heart. When we got back to the police station, we should have been relieved that the day was over. However, knowing that we had to be back again the next day to say goodbye to Fiona was petrifying.

Thursday 4th October 2012. Up again at the crack of dawn, after having next to no sleep at all, we put on our best uniform once again. Shirt ironed, pants pressed, and boots polished, we set off for the final day in this long, painful journey. Again, we boarded the coaches, and as we made our way into the city, I expected to see a lot less officers lining the streets and a lot less members of the public, due to the turn out the day before. As we neared the route to the cathedral I gasped. There again were thousands and thousands of officers in full uniform lining the streets, saluting as we passed; behind them were thousands of members of the public. Not one person blocked our way, extremely respectful. Thank you, you made another horrendous day a little easier to deal with.

When we arrived, we were shown to our seats and awaited the arrival of Fiona. Again, when she entered the cathedral, her hat was balancing on top of her coffin. Again, my legs buckled. I just couldn't get it straight in my head. I was out with her only a few weeks before, having a good laugh and now she lay lifeless in a wooden box, put there by a callous, evil killer. Once she had been taken to her final resting place and we left the cathedral, I felt totally drained and exhausted. My partner and I took it in turns to sleep, in between caring for our children.

PC NICOLA HUGHES and PC FIONA BONE will be remembered

forever by thousands, as for me, they are imprinted on my heart and soul. Rest in peace ladies, I will never forget the ultimate sacrifice that you both made.

I hoped and prayed that this would be the last time I experienced the loss of this type, but again I was wrong.

During the following year, many functions and fund raisers were held in memory of the girls. Nicola's dad, Bryn Hughes, set up THE PC NICOLA HUGHES MEMORIAL FUND. This is a charity who now provide learning opportunities and pre-employment skills in the form of support through grants or services to children (under 21) who have suffered the tragic loss of a close family member through a violent crime, such as murder or manslaughter.

I attended a charity event at The Village Hotel in Ashton under Lyne during 2013 with fellow colleagues. It was a brilliant night, raising lots of money from the ticket sales and auctions. I remember chatting and dancing away with many colleagues, including a beautiful lady, Tracey Miskell.

Tracey was older than me and much wiser, she was giving me life advice over a drink or two and pointing me in the right direction. Tracey had a massive personality and could light up any room with her smile. At forty two years of age, she was youthful, fit and healthy; regularly attending the local gym. You knew when Tracey was on the radio or nearby, due to her loud assertive Scouse accent. She was beautiful, inside and out. But she was most definitely not a lady you would want to mess with.

On September 13th 2013, I was at home; it was my daughter's birthday and I was sitting in the living room, watching her open her birthday presents. My phone kept ringing, but I ignored it as I didn't want to spoil her moment, so let it ring out. My fella's phone started to ring and I was starting to get annoyed that someone just couldn't wait until our daughter had opened her presents. He answered the call, leaving the room so not to disturb the fun. When he came back into the room his complexion had gone very pale and I could see he had tears in his eyes. I wanted to know what was the matter and who was on the phone, but he refused to tell me whilst the presents were being opened. I checked my phone and saw that the missed calls were from work. My mind went into overdrive, after the past year and it almost being the anniversary of Nicola's and Fiona's deaths, I kept thinking the worst and began to panic. I thought the most obscure things could have happened, the cretin could have escaped from custody and was on the rampage again? His family had killed another cop? I didn't know what to think, other than the worst things imaginable. Seeing the panic on my face, my fella took me into another room. He told me that Tracey Miskell, at only forty two years of age, had died. She had died the day before, suddenly without warning. Wow, this was a complete shock; the news had come out of nowhere and I felt like I had been punched, square in the stomach with all my breath leaving my chest. I faintly heard a sob escape from my chest and I sat in silence, hot tears running down my face, in an attempt not to alert the kids to my sudden change in mood. I felt frozen, I didn't know what to say or do. I knew her husband, as he was one of our Sergeants and I felt totally gutted for him and his family.

I attended the police station on September 18th 2013 for the first anniversary of Nicola and Fiona's tragic deaths. A memorial service was being held for them. It made an already devastating day a little harder to manage, knowing that the very next day, we had to go and say our final goodbyes to another beautiful officer taken too early.

On September 19th 2013, my partner and I attended Our Lady and the Apostles Roman Catholic church in Shaw Heath, Stockport. The service was beautiful and the church was filled with police officers and her family. Here, we grieved the loss of yet another friend and colleague, tears silently falling down our cheeks. REST IN PEACE TRACEY, you never ceased to put a smile on my face.

In such a short space of time, I, along with all my colleagues, had felt the full force of death on such a personal level. Whilst dealing with the personal emotions of each individual loss, we had to put on a brave face and get back to serving the public. Many officers were tested at times, when arresting drunks or generally unpleasant people, who were anti police, who revelled in trying to wind up the cops with speeches of how "CREGAN IS A LEGEND", "THANK GOD CREGAN KILLED THEM DIRTY COPS" etc etc. Now police officers are human beings and all have their breaking point, but at no point did I see any officer rise to these idiots. They continued with their job and maintained professionalism. I had been subjected to such a drunken goon who threatened me with all sorts. He told me varying things he would do to my family and then began to declare how god-like Cregan was. It did upset me and yes I did want to rip his tiny head from his shoulders; however, I arrested him for a public order offence and he was charged with the same. Any job is difficult when dealing with the loss of a colleague; however, I believe from experience that being on the front line such as police officer, paramedic or firefighter, the test is a little bit harder.

Many officers suffered and dealt with the loss of Nicola and Fiona silently, in their own way, hoping the pain would pass. I cannot begin to imagine how the officers who were first on the scene to them felt. Having to see your friends in such a horrific manner and knowing it was your job to try and save them but also knowing that you couldn't, how do you live with that?

Waking up every day with those images in your head, that's if you had managed to even sleep at all. Questions swimming around your head drowning you. What if? What if I had taken that job instead? What if I had gotten to them a little faster? What if? What if? What if? Constantly blaming yourself for things that you could never have foreseen, for things that you could never have done. Constantly thinking that you were in some way to blame for something that was completely out of your control. For some, those demons became a little bit easier to deal with. For others, that constant feeling of guilt and self-loathing due to the blame just got too much.

On Tuesday 30th August 2016, I was away on holiday with my family and our best friends. My partner received a phone call which made the colour drain from his face. I, unfortunately, have seen this far too many times before and knew he had been told bad news. I couldn't hear what was being said, so I busied myself with the children. When he finished the call, he came over and out of ear shot of the children, told me that our friend and ex colleague Andrew Summerscales had lost his battle with his demons and had taken his own life.

Devastated was an understatement. Again, that familiar feeling of hot, wet tears running down my face appeared and there was nothing I could do to stop it. I tried to hide it from the kids, but I just couldn't stop it. I had to tell them that I had got a fly in my eye and my friends ushered them away from us for a while.

My partner and I talked it out, I felt so sad for Andrew's family. His son and parents must be so devastated. I then felt angry that four years on, that one-eyed little cretin still had the capacity to affect so many people's lives. I felt an emptiness in my stomach that rose into a panic into my chest. Then I began to think of Andy and what I had known of him. He was forty six years old and had the mental age of a twenty-year-old. He was kind and compassionate, a quiet man who kept himself to himself. When I first met him he petrified me, he was so tall compared to me. He was quiet and I couldn't work out if he was plainly arrogant, or shy, or just didn't like me. When Andy and my fella started working together, their friendship grew and that's when I got to know the real Andy. He literally would do anything for anybody. He had a funny way of knowing if you needed him. He was an honourable and trustworthy friend to my fella, attending our son's christening and most of our family get-togethers. He made it his business to attend my events that myself and my partner competed in, despite it setting him back a fair few quid. When he got wind that I was on another of my missions, and this time had convinced my fella that having chickens in the back garden was a great idea, he mucked in and offered to help.

He was good with his hands and a dab hand at making things with wood, so when we needed a small gate making for the chicken's area, he went quiet on a night shift at work and made us one out of spare wood in his garden! He was well known for his eclectic taste in vehicles and when I needed help collecting yet another of my impulsive and crazy eBay purchases, Andy came to help.

It still makes me chuckle now, sat writing about it. So, he made me ask for the measurements for the aviary before we set off, to make sure it would definitely fit in the back of his long wheel-based transit van. Being a woman and knowing about these things, I guaranteed him that it would; however, I wasn't too sure. His van was his pride and joy and he had had it all boarded out inside, with carpet laid neatly on the floor. This was for when he and his dogs went camping or travelling. Anyhow, we turned up at this lady's house and he took one look at the dismantled aviary, then at his van, then at me and told me in no uncertain terms that there was no way it would fit in.

I then spent the next half an hour convincing him of all the ways that it would fit inside. I don't for one second think that I convinced him however, I think he got sick of hearing my voice, so to shut me up, conceded and we started lifting big, heavy sides into his van. His face was frozen in a look of anger and disdain the entire time. I tried to lighten the mood with a bit of "TO ME, TO YOU?" Chuckle brothers humour, but it was not going down too well. Despite him being well and truly pissed off, he didn't tell me off once, didn't snap or say one single bad word. Not even when the aviary top ripped a big hole in the boarding of the internal roof of his van, which he had just paid to be done. He was silently pissed off, but didn't complain once and didn't shout.

I did find out afterwards, though, that he spent the next few weeks chewing my partner's ear off about the state of his van. He was a funny bloke and those who knew him knew, that despite his exterior, he blamed himself for many reasons about Nicola and Fiona dying. He blamed himself for not being on the van that day and taking one of their places, for not taking the burglary call instead. He was one of the first officers on the scene and saw the most horrific sight before him. He blamed himself for not being able to do more. Friends, family and colleagues tried to support him and reassure him that there was nothing that he could have done or changed; however, no amount of reassurance would alleviate his guilt or pain. He was chosen to carry the girls' coffins into the cathedral, along with other officers and the ladies' families and assisted in laying them to rest.

Now, after taking his own life, he had set his demons free. He was finally at peace and part of me hopes that he grew his wings the day he died and joined the girls, along with Tracey, on their clouds. Angel wings outstretched, looking over us down on earth.

Andy's death affected me, due to knowing how he died and being so close to him as a family. Every time I closed my eyes, I could see him all alone, feeling like he had nothing left. When I closed my eyes, I could see him left where he died, in the way that he had died, constantly in my dreams, both day and night, he was there every time I closed my eyes. Sleeping didn't come easy for a while.

The day of Andy's funeral arrived and my partner and I attended, neither of us wore police uniform. This was because, despite Andy being a great cop, he had left the job as he knew he didn't enjoy the role any longer. We stood there and watched all his friends on motorbikes escort the hearse up the cemetery driveway, it made me smile. Andy would have loved that. We filed into the small church where there was standing room only; people spilling out the door and down the driveway. The religious guy at the front knew Andy personally, his voice breaking whilst he spoke of the good times he'd spent with Andy reduced my partner and I once again to tears. Then "YOU'LL NEVER WALK ALONE" began to play. Andy loved his Liverpool football team and at last, he was laid to rest in peace.

It was an extremely emotive day, but afterwards I felt different. I felt happy that Andy had made his own decisions and was now at peace, and sad at losing a true gentleman. Rest in peace Andy, you will be truly missed x

CHILD NEGLECT

One of the hardest jobs to deal with, for me, was those involving children. In my opinion, the police service and social services are not very good at working together when it comes to vulnerable children. Social services are heavily reliant on the police service and their duty of care to protect vulnerable people. The usual situation would be for a social worker to ring the police any day just prior to 5pm, their finishing time, and disclose a concern for a family or child. They would then leave for the day and be unreachable to answer any further questions regarding the concern. The police would then have a duty of care to attend the address and deal with any concern that they found.

A few jobs which I have attended have broken my heart. On one occasion, I was on a night shift, due to finish work at 7am. A member of the public rang the call room to say they had seen a young child, no older than two years old, walking the streets alone. Due to the kid's age, we got to the area as fast as we possibly could by using our blue lights and sirens. Every officer on the shift turned out to help us. I was first to arrive and found two young children at the back of some houses dressed in a nappy. One was lucky enough to be wearing a thin, sleeveless, cotton vest. The youngest looked to be about eighteen months old and the eldest approximately two and a half. I approached them and asked where they lived. They pointed to one of the houses on the row that had its patio doors slightly ajar. I took them inside to the warm and noticed how dirty they were. Their hair was all matted and unwashed and their hands and feet were filthy. When I took them inside, we entered the rear room of the house. There were blankets pinned up against the patio doors to block out the light and the floor was hidden under rotting rubbish and various broken toys. Venturing into what looked like the living room, I saw a small, ripped sofa in front of a TV which was switched onto a cartoon channel. In front of the TV was a smaller baby that looked to be about ten months old. Again, another blanket was up against this window. Used nappies were strewn about the floor, filled with rotting faeces, and the kids were wandering about, not batting an eyelid, due to it being the norm for them. In the kitchen, the cupboards were empty, the fridge was empty and these kids didn't have anything at all to eat or drink. The sides of the kitchen were piled high with greasy, dirty pots; the cooker was thick with dust and hadn't been used in years, and there was no sign of a microwave or toaster. Still, there was no sign of any adults present in the house, until I heard a loud thundering down the stairs. A bloke appeared in nothing but his boxer shorts, he was about thirty years old and looked like he had just woken up. He was a big guy and was looking pretty pissed off that two police officers were stood in his living room. He demanded to know what the hell we were doing in his house and I attempted to explain that his children had been walking the streets in the freezing cold, with next to no clothes on. I explained that I had come inside to check that they were OK and that nothing bad had happened to their parents. A female appeared from upstairs, wrapped in an old, dirty dressing gown and looked all dishevelled, like she had just woken from a deep sleep. She started panicking that I was there and said that the lock on the back door was faulty, so the kids must have sneaked downstairs whilst they were still asleep and then let themselves out.

I explained that more steps should be taken to ensure the children cannot get out of the house, as anything could have happened to them. I asked about the state of the house and the lack of food. I explained that I would have to inform social services, as it appeared that the family needed some sort of help and assistance. I requested my supervision to attend, along with the child protection team. In the interim, I went upstairs to check up there, and found the bathroom to be filthy. The bath was thick with dust and stains and appeared not to have been used in a long time. The toilet had never been cleaned and stunk badly. The children had no bedding on their beds and on the wall next to the top bunkbed, there was an electric socket hanging from the wall, all the wires were hanging bare. There were more filled nappies strewn around the bedroom, with faeces-stained clothing on the floor. The baby appeared to have nowhere to sleep and when asked, the female said that he slept in her bed with her.

I explained that the children's standard of living fell well below what was expected, they appeared to be malnourished and unclean and didn't have adequate heating, clothing or food. The house was in such a bad state, I wouldn't have allowed an animal to live there. I had started to take photographs of the scene that I was met with. Due to police officers not being given any form of camera, I had to use my mobile phone. Whilst I was doing this, the male of the house snatched the mobile phone from my hands and told me that he would smash it up if I didn't stop. I tried to calm the situation down and the female approached me, in tears. She explained that she suffered from severe depression and anxiety, and had little or no help from friends and family. She struggled with the children and keeping the house in check, and explained that it had spiralled out of control and she couldn't get back on top of it.

Social services and the police child protection team arrived and agreed between them that the family needed support. They gave the parents the ultimatum that they had to find somebody to take care of the children whilst they tidied the house. The kids were shipped off to their grandparent's house and the parents were given two days to rectify the situation. Two days later when the revisit was conducted, the house looked like a different place all together. The beds were all made up with fresh, clean bedding, the house was clean and there was food in the fridge and cupboards; the cooker had been cleaned and they had invested in a microwave. The children were returned to their parents and from that point on, the family received regular support from social services and the child protection team.

On another occasion, the police received a phone call from a concerned shop owner stating that it was 8.30am and a lady had just been in her shop to purchase a bottle of vodka. She said the lady was already 'half cut' and she had two toddlers in her car, who were not strapped into their seats. The lady in the shop had obtained the registration number of the car and I was given the job. I went to the address that the car was registered to and located a very drunk lady. I asked if I could come into her flat, she refused. I explained that I was concerned for the welfare of her children. I explained that I was going to be coming into her flat to check on them, so would like to do that amicably. As I entered, I found the flat to be in a clean and immaculate state. The children were well dressed and their rooms were clean and packed with toys. There was ample food in the fridge and cupboards, but many empty bottles of vodka littered about in the cupboards and bins. I explained to the lady that, due to how drunk she was, I was concerned that she wouldn't be able to care for her children properly. I asked her if she had any friends or family that could help her and look after the children whilst she sobered up. She was an emotionally broken woman. She had suffered domestic violence at the hands of her ex-partner for years. He had assaulted her that badly at several points, she had been put in intensive care. She had managed to escape and the police and social services had rehoused her, out of the area with her two children. Whilst in her new flat, she was completely isolated from friends and family, and spiralled into depression. She got up every day and cared for her children, tidied her flat and managed to get through the day by drinking copious amounts of vodka. She had no one to turn to and didn't know what else to do, so drank until she felt numb. Eventually, I decided to take the children into my care, just until she sobered up. A neighbour agreed to sit in with her and give her coffee and food. Social services were informed and agreed that this lady needed support, rather than her children removing permanently. I took the kids back to the police station whilst we waited for social services. They were beautiful kids with happy personalities. The youngest was sat on my knee on the way back to the station and once at the station, remained close to me until I noticed that his hair was moving. On closer inspection, the poor kid had thousands of tiny lice running around his head, as did his sister. These had been untreated for some time. I informed the social worker when they eventually arrived to collect the children. The kids were returned to their mother as soon as she was sober and, with the help and support of professional services, she managed to control her depression and alcoholism and care for her children properly.

The incidents described above were a result of people's isolation and lack of parenting knowledge. During my policing career, I came to understand that in many poor social areas, families start to reproduce early, due to boredom and lack of knowledge about contraception. Many people who do not work, and claim benefits, raise their children with no work ethic, meaning it is a vicious circle. Young kids become pregnant and have their children early on in life; however, they have never been taught how to cook, clean, read or write. They have never had rules or boundaries so have no idea how to teach their own children or even care properly for them.

It used to piss me off when I went into a house where the kids had minimal toys, dirty clothes and nappies that hadn't been changed for hours on end, but their parents managed to fill their fridge with alcohol and have cigarettes in multipacks. The kids would be dumped in front of the TV all day to watch cartoons whilst their parents slept off their hangovers or drug-induced come downs. These kids could barely speak and didn't bat an eyelid that a police officer was in their house. Mostly, in my role, I became hardened to the incidents that I was faced with; however, child neglect was something that I couldn't understand. In my head, I couldn't imagine why they would procreate if they had no intention of caring for these vulnerable babies. Each and every time I had to utilise my police protection power, I immediately wanted to take the kids home with me. I wanted to rescue them all. Especially the babies. Colleagues knew this and would bring the tiny babies to me if they had to keep them safe at the police station. I would then feed and change them. It would break my heart when I'd find them covered in nappy rash or when their clothes reeked of cigarette smoke. Even more when the kid stank of cannabis. I've sat with babies and toddlers in the children's ward, who are covered in bruises and unexplained injuries, and wanted to get my hands on the monsters that had caused harm to these innocent babies. I never became hardened to neglected children and if I had my own way, I would have taken them all home and looked after them properly.

FOOTBALL

When I first joined GMP, football overtime was an enjoyable shift that most officers were happy to do. If they required more officers at short notice, you would get paid double time. If not, it was time and a half and a good 10-hour shift, with the possibility of being kept on longer to earn more overtime. We policed Manchester United and Manchester City's matches, that was paid for by the clubs. According to figures I located on the internet (that were obtained from using the Freedom of Information Act) last season, GMP were paid £925,126.61 by Manchester United and £944,000 by Manchester City. One would assume that if GMP are charging and receiving this much money that the officers on the ground who policed these events would benefit from the overtime. This is not the case at all.

GMP have reduced the amount of officers that police each event. The shifts of officers have been shortened from 10 hour shifts to 6 hour shifts, and double time is a thing of the distant past. Officers now get paid time and a half – if they are lucky – on their days off. For the unlucky officers their rest days (days off) are often cancelled. This means that they are forced to work the football without being paid and being reallocated another day off at a later time. These cancelled rest days should only really be enforced in cases of extreme circumstances but actually get used for dates such as derby days, that are planned well in advance. So, if the officers are being paid pennies and there are a lot less working the football, where does the rest of that huge sum of money go?

I have worked many football matches in my career, most of which were normal shifts where not much happened, other than standing at a point, taking alcohol off cheeky supporters, having your bum pinched on the concourse by the drunk supporters and posing for pictures with the family supporters. Two which ones that spring to mind, were days I attended my shift, being paid time and a half and earned my wage.

As a level 2 public order trained officer, you are trained to a national level of how to deal with mass disorder. Forming part of a team or PSU as it's named in the cops. Each PSU is made up of one Inspector, three Sgts and twenty one police officers. All these people are spread out over 3 police carriers. All officers in the carrier will have access to a small, round shield, a large, long shield and their full riot, flameproof, protective clothing. This clothing consists of: flameproof under garments, a flameproof balaclava, leg pads, knee pads, thigh pads, body armour (standard issue), arm pads, shoulder pads and a NATO helmet. For short officers like me, there is no specific kit, you just have to cut a bit off your leg pads at the bottom and your arm pads too.

Even if the top, senior, leadership team have specific intelligence to say that there is going to be a mass disorder at a football match, officers on duty are told to wear their normal day uniform, rather than their protective clothing, through fear of the police appearing overly oppressive. That said, officers are sent into football grounds knowing that it could "kick off", into crowds of tens of thousands of people, whilst having to leave their protective equipment in their bags back in the van. The only time that you are allowed to wear your protective clothing is if the bosses give the order to 'suit up'.

On 14th May 2008, I experienced first-hand one of the worst examples of football hooliganism and mass disorder whilst working on the front line. The football match was the UEFA cup final between the Scottish team Rangers and Zenit Saint Petersburg. It was to be played in the city. The policing operation was planned weeks in advance. Pretty much every officer in Greater Manchester, that was fit for front-line duties, was on duty. Many of these officers had had their rest days cancelled, only a few were getting paid.

The Intelligence was such that we already knew a massive number of Rangers fans were descending on the city without tickets for the scheduled game. To plan for this, Manchester City council erected large screens in Manchester Piccadilly Gardens, Albert Square and at the Manchester Velodrome to show the game. The council also erected large, metal fences around these areas, to create sterile alcohol-drinking zones, that were exempt on the day, from the local, no drinking, bylaws of the city. What the police and council didn't envisage is the sheer numbers that descended on the city. 200,000 Rangers fans began to arrive from as early as 7am.

I started my shift at 7am, and paraded on at a designated police station to receive our Intelligence briefing. We were a Level 2 PSU serial and had all our protective clothing and equipment stored in the van. We were told that we had to wear normal day uniform for the tour of duty. This consisted of pants, shirts, body armour, utility belt, hi-vis and bowler hat for the ladies, tit hat for the lads.

Our PSU serial was posted in Albert Square. The Inspector split the serial into three. One van on each of the Alcohol Zone entrances, our serial were the roaming patrols, tasked with speaking to people in and around the metal fences. As it approached late morning, the sun was beaming down and the atmosphere was jovial. We were melting in our thick hi-vis jackets and due to the weather, more and more people kept arriving. Soon the alcohol safety area, where the big screen was situated, was full to the brim and families and supporters started to set up camp on the grass verges on the outer edge of the metal fences. People came in their thousands and spread out over every foot of available space, all drinking alcohol. At first, we were instructed to enforce the No Alcohol Bylaws. There was one Sergeant, one Inspector and seven Police Constables in our serial, we were outnumbered almost 1000 to 1. There were people drinking everywhere. Mostly, they were in good spirits, people sat on pavements, grass verges, walls, spilling out of pubs, down alleyways, there wasn't a single space to move. We were tasked with walking through the crowds, ensuring all was well. There were crowds of men, women and children, all in their blue Rangers kits, with their noses painted blue. The fans seemed to be happy and very pro police. I was stopped every few yards by a jovial fan for a photograph or 500 and the fans revelled in painting the cops' noses in blue.

We all had our police radios but with so many officers on one channel (with the facility of only one speaking at once) it was destined to fail and the radios were rendered useless. I did, on several occasions, ask on the radio for the council to come along and empty the overflowing bins. I also asked them to possibly sweep the streets of all the glass bottles that were gathering in gutters and piling up on the kerbs. Many officers had made the same request, as we were aware that this number of bottles and beer cans and general rubbish would definitely cause problems for the policing of the city in the evening, when fans were a little more inebriated. I was told that the requests had been made to the council on several occasions, but they had refused to attend and clean up.

During the match, floods and floods of people started running towards our location in Albert Square. We were told by the fans that something had gone wrong with the big screen in Piccadilly Gardens and it had gone off. We were warned that thousands of fans were running our way. As they started to arrive the Alcohol Zone became jam-packed. The fans, fuelled by alcohol, were no longer in a good-humoured mood. They believed that the police had purposely turned off the big screen in Piccadilly, so they were well beyond pissed off with us. Pack mentality set in and gangs of people began pushing the fences to get in to see the big screen. The council had hired private security to maintain order at the gates and the police were there to back them up, but chaos broke out.

This was the turning point of the day; this was the point when the atmosphere turned sour. Officers began pressing their emergency buttons, one after another, after another. The radio operators couldn't cope. Luckily, we heard and recognised some of the urgent calls from the part of our serial on the gates. We began to run to them, unsure of what we were going to, unsure of how many people we would face. We were still in normal day uniform and when we arrived, we were vastly outnumbered. A large, angry mob had gathered at the gates and fences. Police officers and security guards stood behind them trying to stop the fences falling on the people inside. The mob on the outside had clubbed together and began pushing and forcing the metal fences down so they could get in; this was done with a complete disregard for the officers who now found themselves trapped under the heavy, falling metal fences.

When faced with a scene such as that, a million things run through your head, but you literally go into auto pilot. Your own safety is not a factor in your decisions, you simply want to help your colleagues and get them to safety. Myself and about seven other officers started grabbing bodies, shoving them away from fences, shifting them from side to side in any attempt to free the trapped officers and private security guards. It took what felt like a lifetime to get to them, but finally we managed to help them out and our Inspector issued the order to get back to our police vehicles as soon as we possibly could. Adrenaline pumping, we hurried back to the vans. Luckily, our serial arrived back at the vehicles uninjured and safe; however, we could still hear emergency buttons being pressed every few seconds, from various officers, and the radio operators couldn't get on to give their locations to get help to them, they were stranded and needed help, but no help was coming.

The Inspector on our serial was a female, neighbourhood Inspector, I had not worked for her before, but knew that she was well respected by many staff on the division. She was very quietly spoken and a lady who treated you with respect, regardless of rank or service length. Due to her kind, quiet nature, you would assume that in a potential mass disorder situation, she would panic. I was very wrong about her. Without this Inspector's quick thinking and calm nature, I believe that myself and other officers may have easily become stranded and injured. I believe that I owe my safety on that day, to this lady.

Once we were safe inside the police vehicles it was clear that the disorder that was going on around us was becoming increasingly violent and more people were joining the large groups that were causing problems.

Our Inspector, at that point, was not in contact with any other senior officers, so looking after her own staff's safety, she finally ordered us to fully 'kit up'. This meant that in the smallest space possible, seven officers (both male and female) had to remove their hi-vis jackets, body armour and clothing, then put on their flame-proof undergarments, flameproof overalls, body armour, arm pads, leg pads. This was a feat in itself, there were legs, arms, arses and heads everywhere, bits of kit flying from one side of the van to the other. We began to get changed whilst parked in the area of Albert Square, but the fans began to rock the police van and the driver made the decision to drive off. Turning on the blue lights and sirens, we travelled to the designated RVP area of Central Retail park on Great Ancoats Street. On our arrival, with a little adjustment, our entire serial was ready to go. Sat in place, with our shields in front of us and NATO helmets on our laps, we were ready to deploy and help in any way we could.

By this time, it was dark and we had been on duty for over twelve hours. There were hundreds of officers from the vans, trying to get their PSU kits on. With no toilets, all the male officers were forming lines up against any spare space of wall, urinating after twelve hours of having to hold it in. The women queued for the only security guard's toilet, that stank to high heaven, but was better than squatting in a bush. We had been provided with a packed lunch at the start of our shift. This consisted of a sandwich, bar of chocolate, bag of crisps, and a bottle of water. This had been long eaten and officers were beginning to feel hungry. With most officers having been pulled out of the city centre, we could once again hear what was going on via the radio. It was terrifying to hear that certain officers had become stranded in the city; I could hear them screaming and begging for someone to come and help. I looked around and it was clear to see that we all felt the same. We didn't care how long we had been on duty, or how little we had eaten, we were ready to go back into the city to retake the streets and help the stranded officers. We were ready there and then, but nobody was moving. We asked our Inspector countless times when we could go and help the officers but she had to wait from the command for the senior leadership team.

In the police, it seems like common sense goes out of the window, there were officers in desperate need of our help and we had hundreds of officers fully kitted up, ready to go and help them. We were not allowed to go anywhere, as the senior leadership team were having a planning meeting, none of them willing to make a bloody decision between them. This meeting took far too long and we could have gone to the aid of the injured officers much sooner than we did.

After what felt like a lifetime, a request was put out over the radio, for a full PSU serial to accompany an ambulance down Newton Street into Piccadilly, to assist locating and rescuing an injured person. My Inspector was the first to volunteer as we were all fully kitted up and were desperate to get stuck in and help. We were thankful to her for volunteering us. We set off in our vans, in a convoy, with the ambulance between us. My van was at the front of the convoy and when we were half way down Newton Street, the van stopped near to a car that had been set on fire. We thought that this was where the injured party was, we alighted the van in the way we were trained, NATO helmets on, long shields carried high,

ONE OUT,

TWO OUT,

THREE OUT,

FOUR OUT,

FIVE OUT,

SIX OUT,

SEVEN OUT

We were stacked along the van for protection, in a straight line. Within seconds of being out of the van, CCTV updated us that we were in the wrong place, so like keystone cops, we reversed the procedure

ONE IN,

TWO IN,

THREE IN,

FOUR IN,

FIVE IN,

SIX IN,

SEVEN IN

Sounds simple, but each with a six foot long shield and in full riot gear, it was very difficult. We travelled to the end of Newton Street and landed at the junction of Piccadilly Gardens. It looked like Beirut. The floor was shining and crunching under the carriers' tyres, a thick layer of glass lined the floor. Smoke filled the air from the cars that had been set alight and there were hundreds of people everywhere. Just before we stopped, we had been given the order of getting out in a professional, safe manner, then staying as a team to assist the Tactical Aid officers whilst the injured person was seen to by the ambulance staff. In that second I was scared. I never thought that I would be, scared that is, but despite the adrenaline pumping through my veins, I was petrified. We located the injured man and surrounded him with our shields held high. I felt completely insignificant and very small at that moment, petrified at the sight of a crowd of hundreds of people charging towards us, hitting anyone in a police uniform. Random people picking up anything that wasn't nailed down and throwing it in our direction. I heard an officer shout *missiles* just prior to feeling a large brick strike me on my helmet. The helmet took the impact, but it still shook my brain and hurt. The feeling I was having was alien. Adrenaline, fear and sense of duty to protect the guy on the floor. I had all my attention focused on protecting the lad on the floor, so I hadn't noticed that he had been lifted quickly into the back of the ambulance and they had driven away.

I felt a tap on my shoulder and I was guided by an officer I didn't recognise as being part of my serial, to assist in forming a line across the junction at Piccadilly. It was an extremely sparse line of officers, faced with hundreds of angry rioters. I saw a very large object coming towards me, as I shouted, "MISSILE" it hit my legs and I realised it was a large wheelie bin.

Some officers in the line had their small, round shields and their batons drawn, whilst others like me, had their long, rectangular shields. I am only five feet four and struggled to lift the shield off the floor. I remember a Sergeant running along the line behind us. He was screaming orders over the sound of the crowd. I'm sure he thought he was William Wallace out of Braveheart. He ran up and down, back and forth shouting about retaking the streets, restoring order and dispersing the crowds. He was trying to instil confidence into the small number of officers he had on his line, to advance towards the crowds of angry rioters who still had many missiles to throw towards us.

I knew in the next few minutes that we would have to advance towards the crowds, in an attempt to disperse them. Missiles such as bricks and glass bottles were still being thrown at the line of officers, but in a short space of time I became unfazed by it. I was aware of rioters at the front of us in a large mob. There were rioters to each side of us, with mobile phones out, filming the scenes as they played out. Completely vulnerable to the rear of our line, I almost shit my pants when I was tapped on my shoulder from behind. Panicking, expecting an angry rioter to be there ready to strike, I turned quickly to see the best sight I could ever have imagined at that point. Lines and lines and lines of officers, kitted up in full riot gear, had joined us. All that I could see, were cops in every direction, hundreds of cops. It was the best feeling ever and as a group, we began to move forwards.

As we advanced in full riot gear, carrying large, full-length shields; some officers had round shields and batons drawn, and loud, clear verbal commands were being shouted by every single officer. "GET BACK, MOVE, GET BACK." Rioters refusing to move were dealt with, meaning when they came at the advancing officers, refusing to move in an aggressive manner, they were struck and moved to the side. Some fell to the floor, but through fear of being left alone, dealing with them and fear of being badly assaulted, the lines of officers continued to advance forwards, taking each junction as they arrived at it, in the tactical manner in which they had been taught. I was confused why rioters were still stood in front of an advancing line of officers with shields and batons, still throwing missiles at us, still attempting to break through the line to hit or kick us. I was physically exhausted. I asked a big, burly officer who was in the line next to me, if he would swap shields with me. Mine was the long, tall one and weighed a ton. His was a small, round one and was much lighter. I was that exhausted that I was struggling to lift my shield up and despite my request, the officer wasn't too happy at swapping. I didn't care, I was tired and needed a break, so he swapped.

We continued to proceed forwards, asking families to seek shelter and safety in shops and takeaways that were still open. Eventually the crowds dispersed and after becoming split up from their original serials, officers were milling around the city centre in groups, delirious from hunger, fatigue, injury and worry for the other officers. Finally, we managed to piece together the officers from our serial, picking them up from various places around Piccadilly and the Arndale Centre. Whilst doing so, we got the opportunity to survey the scene before us. I found the officer who had my shield and swapped back quickly before finding the other officers.

The floor was thick with broken glass, cars were overturned and on fire, shop windows had been smashed, street furniture was upside down, it was like we were in a war zone. It was 2.30am and we had been on duty for 19½ hours. Tired and hungry, we were driven back to our police stations where we de-kitted and made our way home to our warm, comfy beds. Laying in my bed, it felt surreal that I had just been in the centre of a full-blown riot, and now I was at home, safe and uninjured.

The next day, I switched on the television and watched the scenes of the previous day unfold on the news. Knowing I was right in the middle of the disorder, I felt lucky to be alive, let alone uninjured. Again, I believe I owe my safety on that day to the Inspector of our serial, who made some of the best decisions with her staff in mind.

Approximately one month after these riots, I received an email from the Professional Standards branch of the police. It was a blanket email, addressed to all the officers on duty that day. The email stated that several complaints had been made to the Police Complaints Department, stating that the police had used excessive force that day and one man in particular had been knocked over by an officer, breaking his hip. Obviously, this was extremely unfortunate for him; however, on the evening in question, hundreds of officers were dressed in full riot gear, shouting at the crowds, asking and begging them to get back and to move. Officers, including myself, were guiding genuine members of the public into open shops and shop doorways to avoid any rioter's missiles from hitting them. It is extremely difficult to differentiate between a rioter and another person when they are stood shoulder to shoulder, both shouting and swearing at the cops, both refusing to move, both refusing to disperse or to go home. I know that after being on that front line, not one officer whom I was around at the time used any excessive force. Not one officer intentionally injured any person and it was just unfortunate that this complainant had become injured.

The police are extremely careful about how they allow the media to report on situations like this. They at no point labelled this as a riot. The word 'riot' insinuates that the police have lost control of law and order and as such, are liable to pay for any damage caused by the rioters. In my opinion, this was most definitely a riot, the police withdrew almost completely from the city and allowed the rioters to run amok until they "RETOOK THE STREETS". When we went back into the city, there were overturned cars on fire, shop windows smashed and hundreds of angry people throwing bricks and bottles (and various other things) at the police. In my opinion, this was most definitely a full-scale riot.

I have worked many other football matches since this Rangers game, all passing without any disorder at all. One match however, that sticks in my mind, is a very recent one where Manchester City played Everton at home, at the Etihad stadium in Manchester. It was a late kick-off, so the fans had had an ample amount of time to get sloshed before the game. Our serial was stationed with the away fans and as the match neared its end, Manchester City were winning. This meant that Everton were not going to get their shot at playing their arch rivals Liverpool at Wembley. The Everton fans, at first, seemed to have taken this quite well and began leaving the stadium in an orderly manner. Someone in the police planning department had made a major mistake and had failed to deploy enough officers in the void between the exiting home and away fans. The void was about ten metres in width and thirty metres in length. The City fans lined the small three foot high metal fences on their sides, chanting at the Everton supporters. In the void, there were about seven officers, including myself and my partner, separating these hundreds of chanting fans. The fans soon became wise to the lack of officers. The City fans were chanting at the Everton fans. They were truly winding them up about their loss of the opportunity to play Liverpool at Wembley.

Suddenly, I saw an older guy about forty to fifty years old, break through the barrier on the Everton side. I was the closest officer to him so ran and took hold of him, to stop him from getting any closer to the City fans and run the risk of him being assaulted. This didn't go to plan and the man grabbed hold of me with both of his hands, swung me around, throwing me to the floor in the crowd of angry Everton fans. People began to kick and grab at me and my bowler hat fell off. I panicked and thought that I was a goner but then I felt someone grab me and lift me up. I think that it was a fan and I was extremely grateful to them. As I stumbled to my feet, a lad, mid twenties picked up one of the metal fences and threw it straight at me. When it didn't hit me, he ran forwards, picked it up again (with the assistance of a few other fans this time) and threw it at me again, with considerable force, it struck me in my legs. A few more officers had arrived by now and I could see the bronze Commander stood back, surveying the scene that was rapidly spiralling out of control. He had with him a police constable, whose job it was to take notes of any major decisions he may make on the day. She was a young officer with short blonde hair, walking around carrying a clip board and a pen. I just remember chuckling to myself, as coins and fences were being thrown towards us, she was still attempting to scribe the Commander's words. I leant over and told her that she may want to put her clipboard away and get out her baton. She did just that and suddenly realised exactly how dangerous a situation she had found herself in.

The Tactical Aid officers assisted our serial in forming a line between the fans. We were in normal day uniform, with no protection apart from our body armour, especially now my hat had gone AWOL. I began to feel coins hitting me on my head, and felt the blood trickling in my hair. I literally had no protection at all, the crowds were hundreds strong, hitting, kicking and forcing their way towards the police line. I made the decision to draw my baton, as many other officers did at the same time. I shouted loudly over and over, "GET BACK, GET BACK, GET BACK." As they ignored me and the other officers and moved forwards towards us, I swung my baton towards the violent crowd, hoping it would assist in dispersing them, hoping it would stop them from attacking us anymore. I was really scared. I felt totally vulnerable, as we were completely outnumbered about seventy five to one. I had now been hit a few times by the coins, on my head. The fans, running out of pound coins, had located bigger missiles to throw, such as wooden mops and brushes from their coaches. They began to chant racist chants at the black officers I was stood with. Again, shouting, "GET BACK" I swung my baton again, this time striking two or three people. They still wouldn't move. That's when the police horses showed up. I heard the order faintly to part and let the horses through. As they made their way into the crowds, they were that close that they brushed past my shoulder on the way in.

I thought that at least the horses would put the crowd off and disperse them, but I was gobsmacked at the scenes that unfolded. I saw some fans punch the horses to their faces and bodies. These people were vile; eventually, we managed to get them all back onto their coaches and escort the coaches away from the city, leaving the injured officers and horses behind.

This football game was the perfect example of how the end result of a match can totally change the atmosphere of fans, and how disorder is mostly unplanned mayhem, initiated by a few individuals intent on causing trouble. On this day, I believe I was very lucky to get home with minimal injuries. This was the final match I worked at before I left the force.

POLICE ASSAULTS

When I first joined the cops, I was trained to defend myself using a list of 'Home Office approved' techniques. These comprised of: open hand defence tactics, verbal communications, and learning how to use my baton, CS spray and handcuffs. After ten years of dealing with violent people, I soon came to realise that when it came down to it, you used whatever you could to protect yourself. Home Office approved techniques just didn't cut it in the real world. In August 2013, I joined a local kickboxing gym to lose weight, and learned several self-defence techniques. As I progressed further in my learning, I felt more confident in dealing with situations whilst at work. I was able to confidently communicate with violent and angry people and calm them down without using any force whatsoever. There were a few occasions where my verbal communications didn't work because the person was either high on drink or drugs.

On one occasion, we got a call from a petrified woman that her ex-partner was trying to get into her house. He had put his hand through the window and when we arrived, there was blood everywhere. The guy was bladdered and high as a kite on cocaine. He seemed to calm down whilst I spoke with him, so I placed him in handcuffs and got him to stand with his back against my police car. My colleague went inside to check on the lady and her children whilst I stayed with the male, trying to engage him in conversation. His mood was erratic, and out of nowhere, he lunged forward and headbutted me. I shouted for my colleague's help and she ran out of the front door and down the garden path like Miss Trunchbull from *Matilda*, rugby-tackling him and taking him to the floor. Whilst on the floor, the man started to struggle violently, kicking out and trying to bite us. My colleague reached across and pressed the emergency button on my radio, as hers wasn't working. The closest patrol was ten minutes away. This feels like a lifetime when you're trying to restrain a violent man, twice your size. The bloke trying to get away was kicking us and trying to bite and headbutt us, so I used my CS spray and sprayed him. It didn't affect him at all and left me and my colleague spluttering and choking on the fumes; snot dripping from our noses and tears streaming from our eyes. Eventually, when back up arrived, we were a mess, suffering the effects of CS spray, covered in the man's blood and mud from the floor. I ended up with bruises on my head from the headbutt and bruises all over my arms and legs from his kicks and the scuffle. He was arrested for police assault, along with the criminal damage to the property. In the morning when he was interviewed, he was cleared of the damage as it was his property. He was given a police caution for the police assault as he had no previous convictions. This meant he got told not to do it again. No court appearance, no criminal record for headbutting a female police officer and causing bruises all over my body. I was livid. I had to go home to my little girl and explain why mummy had bruises on her face and this man had received a simple warning.

On another occasion, I was standing at the scene of a serious assault with my colleague, when a car drove past us at about 3am with seven people on board and no lights on. It was swerving all over the road, so we made a quick decision to leave the scene and go and stop the car, to prevent them from killing anyone. We jumped into the police van and my colleague put on the blue lights and sirens and tried to pull the car over. Surprisingly, the driver didn't ignore us, and pulled over straight away. When he got out, it was clear that he was very drunk, and failed the roadside breath test. He was arrested and placed in the rear of our police van. The car, which belonged to his grandmother, was parked and locked up on the side of the road and all his drunken friends were sent on their way, to walk home. They were not very happy about walking and tried to argue that they were, in fact, sober enough to drive. This was not the case, so we left them walking away and we transported the male to custody. As we were travelling towards the police station, another call came in from a neighbour located where we had just left the drink driver's car. The neighbour stated that the group of people we had just left were attempting to break into the car and drive it away. With our prisoner still in the back of the van, we swung it around and made our way back. The description of the main offender was: white male, large, muscular build with a shaven head, wearing jeans and a white t-shirt. We drove past the car, which now had its driver's door bent back, and located the males a short distance away. The main offender stuck out like a sore thumb, so as my colleague pulled alongside him, I jumped out of the passenger side of the van and took hold of him by his wrist. I told him that he was under arrest for the damage to the car. Using no effort at all, he picked me up, lifting me clean off the floor, and threw me as hard as he could against the police van. I fell to the floor, winded and dazed. He ran off towards the main road, with my colleague in hot pursuit. A scuffle ensued between the pair, and the male started swinging wild punches at my colleague. Within seconds, the lad ran back towards me as his shirt was ripped clean off him by my colleague. I just saw this massive guy running towards, me who had already managed to take the wind out of me, and knew I had no chance of restraining him on my own. He was clearly drunk and his increased strength made me believe he had been taking a drug such as cocaine too. As he approached me, I put my right leg out and he tripped straight over it, falling face down onto the floor, splitting his head on a car tail pipe. I hoped that this would be the end of the struggle, so I tried to place him in handcuffs, with the help of my colleague. I managed to get one handcuff on his wrist before he began violently struggling again, hitting out, and kicking and headbutting towards us. I used my CS spray and it finally subdued him enough to place him in the handcuffs. I requested an ambulance for him, as he had cracked his head open on the tail pipe, and informed the radio operator what had just happened. I was left winded, bruised and suffering the effects of CS spray, but apart from that my injuries and my colleague's were minimal. This male was charged and went to court, where he was found guilty of police assault. He received a fine and was ordered to pay compensation to both myself and the other officer.

A more recent incident occurred when both myself and a colleague were on a 5pm-3am shift. It was approximately 1.30am and we were driving along one of the main roads in the area which we were based. In the distance, I notice a group of three lads in the middle of the road, pushing and shoving, unsteady on their feet. Given the time of night, I assumed they had just come out of one of the pubs. Craig, my colleague, asked them to shift out of the road, so they didn't get run over. They refused, telling him that it was a free country, so I jumped out and took hold of the ring leader, leading him off the road, trying to reason with him, calm him down and get them all to go home. They started to argue, I told them to stop acting like idiots and go home, and got back in the van. The main drunken fool followed me back around the van, into the middle of the road and argued that I couldn't speak to him in that way. Again, I shifted him out of the road and started to take his details; he became angry and started swinging his arms around in my face. He had been given plenty of chances by this point, so my colleague Craig came over and took hold of him, telling him that he was under arrest for being drunk and disorderly in a public place. He had placed one handcuff on the lad's hand, when he began to violently struggle. I assisted in restraining him, but this guy was clearly under the influence of something other than alcohol and began kicking out and attempting to bite and headbutt Craig. As a result, I pushed his head back with my palm under his chin to disorientate him. At this point, from out of nowhere, a woman appeared, screaming down my ear like a banshee. She began hitting the back of my head and my back, yelling at me to get off her boyfriend. In the melee, I tried to tell her that he was under arrest but she wasn't listening and continued to hit me. She went to grab my hand away from her boyfriend's chin, so he lunged towards Craig again. With that, I made sure Craig had a good hold of the lad and turned to face the woman, shouting at her to back off and pushing her away from us. The woman came straight back at me, pushing me hard, causing me to stumble backwards. At this point, she had gone well beyond the point of reasonable behaviour and I went to take hold of her and told her she was under arrest for assaulting a police officer. As I did, so she swung a big haymaker punch towards my face, I rolled under, grabbed her arm and took her to the floor. This woman was about six feet tall, large build and much stronger than me, so having her on the floor was my safest option. I managed to get one handcuff loosely around her wrist but it wouldn't tighten as she was fighting so violently. Suddenly, out of nowhere, another bloke came over to us and I thought that he had come to help me. I was wrong. This bloke lunged forward and punched me in my face, telling me to get off the woman on the floor. He then took hold of the woman's arm that was in the handcuffs, and started trying to drag her away from me. I knew that if the handcuff came off her wrist, it would be a dangerous weapon against me so I began to punch out at him to try and stop him. I could hear Craig still struggling with the original male and then suddenly, the woman bit down on my left arm. She had managed to get her massive mouth around my entire forearm and was biting it as hard as she possibly could. The pain was unbearable so in sheer panic (and an attempt to get her off me) I punched her as hard as I possibly could in the face three times to get her to let go. I was screaming at her to let go and she still wouldn't. Through the sheer terror that I would have been badly assaulted by both of these people, I managed to press my emergency button. I then got out my CS spray and sprayed both the male and the female. They both stopped their attack and finally, the street filled with cops. I arrested both the male and the female for assaulting me and they were sent to the police station. During the incident, one of the original males who was arguing in the street was walking around, filming the entire thing on his mobile phone. When I was being hit by this grown man, he stood there and filmed, at no point did he attempt to help me. So, when it had all calmed down, I went over to him and seized his phone from him, as it contained evidence of the assaults on me. He was gutted.

I had to attend the local A and E department to get my arm looked at. The woman had damaged all the muscle and tissue in my left forearm, causing bad bruising and swelling. She had broken the skin, so I had to have a hepatitis injection, a tetanus shot and was placed on a course of strong antibiotics for the next two weeks. The day after, I woke up with pins and needles in my arm from the tissue and nerve damage. This lasted weeks and I struggled to assist my children with getting dressed and tying their shoes.

I had arrested the female for a section 18 assault, which is one of the most serious assaults. I did this as she had assaulted me badly, whilst I had been trying to arrest her. Once she had been interviewed, she denied ever biting me and stated that I had attacked her and used excessive force on her. I came back on duty the next day and an officer had taken the evidence to the Crown Prosecution Service, who had reviewed the evidence and had decided to downgrade the assault from a section 18 to a section 39 which is an assault without injury. She would have been eligible to receive a police caution for this. I was fuming. My arm was a mess; I had been attacked by two adults at the same time and this woman looked like she would receive a slap on the wrist. I made my feelings clear and the Inspector on duty at the time reviewed it and appealed the decision on my behalf. The female was sent home on bail and a case was built to show all the evidence from the night, including the CCTV evidence and mobile phone footage.

Eventually, the female was charged with the original section 18 assault and a trial date was set for August the following year, at Manchester Crown court.

Whilst waiting for this trial date, the other male who assaulted me appeared at Magistrates court. He argued that due to his punches towards me not being captured on the CCTV or mobile phone, they mustn't have happened. He said that he would plead guilty to an obstruct police rather than assault police. The prosecution advised me to take that plea, as it carried the exact same sentence as the assault police. I agreed and he left court with a slap on his wrist.

The trial date came the following year. Two days before, I was advised that it was to be adjourned and a new date had been set for August the year after. The three people who had been arrested on the night had all made complaints to the professional standards branch of the police about me for use of excessive force, so for two years I had that looming over my head. Finally, when we attended for the trial at Crown court, the case was heard in front of a judge and jury. I sat in the court room, giving my evidence and being cross-examined by the defence. I was called a liar and a thug for punching his client in the face. I was made to feel like I was the one in the wrong but finally, after all the evidence was heard the jury retired to make their decision. When they returned, they had reached a unanimous decision and found the woman guilty of assaulting me, causing injury whilst attempting to resist arrest. I felt like crying with relief. The worry of the last two years was over. She had a young baby and was of previous good character, so received the minimal sentence. She was given a fine, ordered to pay compensation and had lost her job working with vulnerable people.

The sentence was irrelevant to me at that point, it was just the fact that finally she had been convicted. It was over. I could move on without the complaint looming over me.

POLICE COMPLAINTS

Many old-school bobbies say that if you're not getting complained about, then you're not doing your job properly. I don't know how much I agree with that. However, I do believe that if you are using your powers to take away somebody's right to freedom by placing them under arrest, or if you are taking away their right to a private life by entering their home with a view to search it, then you are going to upset them and be vulnerable to a complaint or two. If you are a lazy bobby who sits doing nothing, then the likelihood of being complained about is very low.

The two people who assaulted me, which I explained previously, had complained that I used excessive force against them. Once they were found guilty in court, the complaint was closed.

I have received my fair share of complaints in my career. Most were resolved locally by the team Inspector and were just people complaining about the way I spoke with them, or my attitude. When a situation is heated, sometimes the only way to speak to a person is in the language that they understand, to get them to register your presence and listen. On many occasions, I have had to raise my voice to people and swear at them. This is using direct verbal communication which, on most occasions, takes their attention away from the original problem thus diffusing the situation and places their focus onto me. Only then have I any chance of calming that person down.

People have complained because, whilst in their house, I have asked the children if they have seen daddy hitting mummy, or mummy hitting daddy. Families don't like the children being questioned, as they tend to tell the truth.

The next level of complaint is, if somebody alleged any criminal charges against an officer such as use of excessive force or misuse of powers. Again, this has been done to me. If an incident involves more than one officer, but it isn't clear which officer it is in relation to, all the people are served with papers. When you are served with papers, you are given a brief outline of the alleged offence and then the Inspector must read out the police caution in full. Treated like a criminal, you are then investigated fully. They then decide if the complaint is true or not, based on the evidence and finally let you know, months or years later. I have never ever been found guilty of any complaint. They have all been falsely made against me over the years, but to have one looming over you is quite scary as it's your job on the line.

I have been 'papered' for silly things, such as a male prisoner said I sexually assaulted him when I placed him in his cell. These days, the custody suites are full of CCTV with audio capabilities, so that complaint didn't go anywhere.

I was complained about by a member of the public to the IPCC because, whilst dealing with a male who had been attacked in a pub, a female approached me and asked what I was talking about. I explained to her that I was dealing with an incident and asked if she would move aside, which she refused to do. She appeared to be one of the friends of the injured male and she had clearly taken a dislike to me. The pub was full of officers, so I went outside, removing myself from the situation. Once outside, she followed me and began to demand my collar number for being so rude to her. She began a tirade of drunken abuse and told me that she paid my wages so she had a right to an explanation from me. Finally bored of her abuse, I spoke with her and asked what she did for a living. When she said she didn't work, I smiled and walked away. Clearly she did not pay my wages, I paid hers. She didn't like this very much and began demanding my number, which she was given. When she sobered up the next day, she wrote in to the IPCC to explain about what a disgrace of an officer I was, and that I degraded her by asking her what she did for a living. I was spoken to at length by my Inspector who then, in turn, spoke back to her. It was locally resolved, meaning she was probably told that I had apologised for my awful behaviour. This was not the case; I wasn't sorry, as I had done nothing wrong. I was simply trying to do my job and this woman, brave from alcohol, began demanding to know how and when and what and where. The complaint went away so I was happy.

One of the longest and most worrying complaints that I had looming over my head was from a lady in her fifties who was claiming that my negligence had caused her auntie's death. Now, being blamed for someone's death is serious, and not only could it result in me losing my job, but also could have resulted in a prison sentence. The incident started when a local nursing home contacted the police and asked for help with a family member of one of the residents. We were told en route to the job that the family member was the niece of the elderly lady. She was causing a scene and attempting to physically pick her aunt up out of bed and remove her from the home.

On my arrival, I was approached by the relative, who started shouting and bawling at me about what my job was, and what I should or shouldn't do in this situation. I asked if the elderly lady required any medical assistance in the form of an ambulance and was told that she didn't as they had on-site nurses who were caring for her at that time. I took all parties, including the manager of the care home and the relative, into the main office so as not to upset any of the other residents. Whilst in there it was explained that the relative was unhappy with the placement for her auntie, as it was too far away from her house. The home manager explained that there is a procedure to follow and a request had to be made through local social services, then the lady had to be seen by a doctor to ensure she was fit to be moved which, in the home's opinion, she was not. I listened to all parties' explanations and then asked if I could go and speak with the lady, who was named Edith. Edith was ninety six years old, confined to her bed and quite poorly, but still was of sound mind. When I went into her room, I introduced myself and explained why I was there. I spoke at length with her and asked her what it was that she wanted, as she was the most important person in this incident. She told me that she was tired, she said that she just wanted to be left in peace. She said that she didn't want to move anywhere and she quite liked it just where she was. I explained to her that I would respect her wishes and left her to rest, returning to the other parties. I told them that Edith wished to be left alone to rest and that the relatives were not to take her anywhere that day. I explained that they had to make the request through social services and that if they returned, causing any more problems, they would be removed to prevent a breach of the peace. It was at this point that the relatives told me that they had phoned an ambulance for their auntie, so that she could be taken into hospital. I pointed out that she had already been seen by a nurse at the home but when the paramedics arrived, I took them to meet Edith. Edith was a little teary as I had promised her that I would let her rest but when I made it clear that the lovely paramedics were here to make her smile, she perked up. The paramedics asked me why they had been contacted and I answered honestly that I didn't know. They examined Edith and said that they were not as qualified as the doctors and nurses at the home, so didn't need to be there. They put across that moving Edith would make her more poorly and most likely be fatal.

When they left, they had Edith laughing and joking with them and I went to tell the family that it had been decided that Edith was staying put until they had followed the correct procedure. We all left the home. The family made sure they told me when they left that I was unfit to be a police officer.

A few weeks later, I was approached by my response Inspector and informed that a serious complaint had been made about me. He said that the relative had complained that whilst I was dealing with the incident, I had cancelled three ambulances that she had contacted, and this had caused her auntie to die a few days later. Luckily, all conversations that are had over the radio with the operators are recorded, meaning if I had cancelled any ambulance, then it would have been on tape. The reason that poor Edith had passed away was, because against all medical advice, her niece had gone through the correct channels and had her moved. Edith died the same day that she arrived at the new home through no fault of mine. It took the Professional Standards officers over twelve months to clear my name of this complaint and the worry I felt over that time was horrendous.

Complaints against police officers are a daily occurrence of any police forces. People complain about processes taking too long and not being updated. Complaints about excess force, complaints against illegal searches, complaints against illegal stop and searches, complaints that cars have been seized, complaints about practically every part of the job that you tried to do. I am happy that, throughout my policing career, any complaint against me was unfounded and that I always strived to be the best police officer that I possibly could. I can't say the same for all the officers I worked with though. Complaints against some were totally justified.

PECULIAR JOBS AND THOSE
THAT MADE ME LAUGH

When you do a job that's twenty four hours a day seven days a week, working alongside people who will ultimately save your life if it came down to it, you become so close that you share a dark sense of humour. This humour allows you to assist one another to deal with the most horrific events, from suicide, death or murder, to child neglect of the worst nature. By having a laugh and a joke about horrific events, you are not intending to be disrespectful to anybody. As a cop, you are making light of something that may be difficult to deal with and by doing this, you are tricking your mind into believing that the incident is less harrowing than it truly is. I guess it's a coping mechanism that you must adopt in order not to go mental.

The other side of the policing role means that you deal with an entire spectrum of modern day society. From the youngest of people to the oldest, from people who got up every day to attend school, college, or work, to those who spent most of their days sleeping and simply surviving. Dealing with the intoxicated or drug-induced people, the mentally-ill or those who were a little bit eccentric.

Every day was different, every job was different, many were serious but some hilarious. A few of the funniest that I can remember are to follow. These are by no means intended to poke fun at any person or to discriminate against them, it just goes some way in explaining how hard it is sometimes to keep a straight face as a professional person.

When I was quite young in service, I was out on my own and was called to an elderly lady who had fallen in her flat and couldn't get back up again, so couldn't get to the door for paramedics. It turned out that the poor lady had been there for a good few hours and had just managed to make her way to a telephone to contact help. On my arrival, another female officer joined me at the flat and between us, we tried to locate an open window, before causing damage to the door by putting it in. Being quite good at climbing, I managed to scale the six foot metal side gate to the property and make my way around the back. The back door was slightly ajar, on a security chain. I kicked the door three or four times, forcing the chain to snap and the door to swing open. I let my colleague know that I had managed to gain entry and went inside with the simple intention of finding the lady and helping her. I was that intent on getting to her quickly that I didn't notice anything different about the flat at all. I went through every room, shouting that I was a police officer and I was there to help, but I couldn't find the lady anywhere. Finally, I heard a faint voice coming from the bedroom, I was confused as I had already checked in there but when I looked on the other side of the small bed, where there was a small gap between the bed and the window, I located her lying on the floor. I was shocked and taken aback as she was a dwarf. She was no more than three feet tall but was an elderly lady. I was shocked as I had never met an elderly person with the dwarf gene before, this is mainly due to their life span being much shorter. I stood, unable to get my words out, stuttering until she shouted at me,

"STOP BLOODY JUST STANDING THERE AND HELP ME!"

I felt so rude, I didn't want to upset the poor lady. I didn't want to hurt her either, so asked her if she wanted me to pick her up. Her reply made me chuckle,

"OF COURSE I BLOODY DO! I CAN'T LIE HERE LIKE AN UPSIDE-DOWN TORTOISE ALL DAY NOW CAN I!"

So with that, I picked her up and put her on her bed. I placed her walking frame next to her and she asked me to leave her alone for a second so she could change her clothes, as she had soiled herself after being there for so long. I went to open the door for my colleague and the paramedics. I tried to explain to them before they entered the house that the lady was a little lady with a massive personality but, one by one as they entered the living room where she was now sitting, they were taken aback. She was a feisty lady and had the paramedics laughing at her jokes. I went to make her a cup of tea and some food whilst she was being medically examined. When I went into the kitchen, I was amazed that it was the same as any other I had been in, but had been adapted to be three feet smaller in height. The lady had steps for her fridge and a lowered cooker to make her completely independent. In the living room, it looked like a scene out of the three bears, there was a massive arm chair, which, she informed me, belonged to her late husband who was of normal height. There was a medium-sized sofa, which she explained that she could just about manoeuvre onto when her mobility was playing ball. Finally, she had the smallest chair out of them all, that matched all the others but had been especially adapted for her. This lady was small in stature but had the most amazing laugh and eccentric personality. By the time we left, she had us all laughing at her flirting with the paramedics.

On another occasion, I was driving a police van along a quiet dark back street in the early hours of a Saturday morning. I spotted a young lad who was about seventeen to eighteen years old, around six feet tall and wearing smart clothes. This made me think that he had been out partying for the evening. The thing that made this guy stand out to me was that he was currently 'army crawling' along the road in the dark, between the parked cars. My first thought was that he may be injured, so I stopped the van and jumped out. I was with another cop, who also got out to offer any assistance. As soon as my colleague got out of the van, the young lad started army-rolling across the floor shouting, "HE'S COMING, HE'S COMING". Well, now I realised that this guy wasn't injured so my next thought was, either he suffered from mental health issues or he was on drugs. Eventually, I managed to calm him down and convince him that we were real police officers and we were there to help him. Whilst speaking to him, he was foaming at his mouth and his pupils were like pin pricks, so I requested an ambulance to check him out. He didn't know his own name, didn't know where he lived or where he had been and, intermittently throughout the conversation, he would army roll off down the street and hide behind a car. It was hard not to laugh at this guy. When the paramedics arrived, they agreed that he was very vulnerable and whisked him away to the local hospital. I wish I could have recorded him and his behaviour, to show the young adults that I came across within my role. This would go some way in explaining exactly why not to use drugs. He could have been robbed or attacked and badly injured.

Another odd incident I went to was a call from a lady to the cops. She was reporting a domestic incident with her husband. From what the call taker could decipher through the barrage of abuse she was receiving, was that this abusive woman had returned home to find her husband in the arms of another woman. When I arrived, I was shouted instructions to let myself into the house, which I did. I entered the living room to find a woman sat on the sofa. Now, I'm not one to judge; however, she knew that the police were on their way and had plenty of time to get dressed.

I'll set the scene for you. The woman was a large female, I'm guessing about 18–19 stone; she was wearing a well-worn white vest top with dinner stains down the front. She had a massive chest with no bra on. Her boobs were hanging out from under the top. She had several thick, gold chains around her neck, which went some way to cover up the prominent stains. She was wearing a long skirt that she had hitched up, to sit cross legged on the sofa. She clearly didn't like wearing underwear as she had failed to put any knickers on either. I didn't know where to look, never mind my male colleague. She sat smoking cigarette after cigarette and started every sentence with, "What it is, right..." She looked sixty five but was only thirty five years old.

She began to explain that her husband had befriended the next-door neighbour. She had allowed her to come around to their house to watch films and have tea together, as she thought that they were just friends. Tonight, she said that she had returned home from work to find them on her sofa in each other's arms, smooching and cuddling. I asked her where they both were now and she said, "I bloody dragged her out of my house and he went running after her like a little bitch."

She told me that they were both currently cowering next door. This woman, surprisingly, didn't appear very upset, she just wanted me to go next door and tell the woman that she was welcome to her husband.

So, off I trotted two yards to the next door and knocked on it. A person answered the door and I couldn't quite work out if it was male or female. So, when I was invited in, I had to take another look and saw that it was a female, wearing a short nightie with no bra (I couldn't understand why none of them liked underwear!). She stood, with her monobrow covering most of the space on her forehead, draping herself inappropriately across the stair rail. She was wearing a dressing gown which she had just opened to reveal her legs, which were so hairy you could barely see her skin. She was smiling like the cat that had gotten the cream. Next door's husband was nowhere to be seen but I could hear rustling around upstairs which I guessed was him.

I asked the woman what had happened and she smiled smugly, replying, "Well, he chose me didn't he?"

Not knowing quite how to move the situation forwards, I began to take details from the woman, so that I could complete the domestic update on the computer when I got back to the police station. I began by asking her for the male's details. She went rather quiet and then admitted that she didn't know his surname, let alone his date of birth, so she shouted him down the stairs. I expected to see when he came down that he would be a stallion of a man, having these two ladies fighting over him; however, I was sadly mistaken. I had to do a double take, as I couldn't understand how the man that stood before me had managed to get himself into this love triangle. He was a man mountain, standing at about six feet five tall and weighing in at about thirty stone. He was sporting a moustache from the 1950s and a mop of dyed, black hair on top of his head. He looked to be about fifty years old. The bottom of his belly was hanging out from beneath his buttoned-up shirt-type pyjama top. He had no socks on and his yellow toe nails were curling over the end of his toes like Quavers. He had a distinct body odour smell and his breath when he talked smelled like a million stale cigarettes. I asked him for his details which he refused to give to me.

I asked him what had happened and he said simply and confidently, "What can I say they both wanted me and I chose her," nodding at the woman who still stood, smiling smugly. I asked him what his intentions were for the future and he said that he intended to move into this house where we were now. I asked him if he had thought it through and told him that it may be a little awkward, with his wife living next door, to which he shrugged and said that she will get over it.

I was speechless and fighting the urge to laugh at his complete brashness and to tell them all to grow up, but I didn't laugh and remained professional. As I was leaving, the bloke asked me to get his uniform for him, so he could attend work the following day. It seemed like a reasonable request, so I agreed. As I made my way next door, he kept adding things to the list that he needed, so in the end, I accompanied him next door to prevent any breach of the peace so he could collect his own belongings. I would have assumed the scorned wife would have stayed in a different room, but again I was wrong. She was adamant that she wanted to pack him off next door, so started to remove his clean clothes from the washer and dryer and pile them up in the hallway, telling him not to bother coming back. As he was walking out of the door, he turned to his wife and asked her if she could grab him his packed lunch for work the following day out of the fridge. I asked him when she went to get it who had made the lunch and he said that his wife had, as it was her job. I had to pick my jaw up from the floor before I told him that he was a cheeky git. He had just been found cheating on his missus and now had the cheek to request the lunch that she had spent time making him. Suffice to say, he didn't receive his lunch. He was packed off back inside next door and advised not to attend the address again that evening.

I went back into the scorned wife's house and was taking the final details for the domestic report. Whilst she was lighting yet another cigarette, I noticed two birds in a cage in the corner of the room, tweeting through the plumes of smoke. I thought to myself that they probably do the same job as the canaries used to do for the miners down the pit. To try and lighten the situation, I asked the woman about the birds, asking if they were Cockatiels. Her reply, in the driest tone she could muster, ruined my professional exterior, "NO THEY'RE LOVE BIRDS". At that point I almost choked, said my goodbyes and turned on my heel with tears of laughter running down my cheeks.

What a totally strange and surreal job that was. It would have fitted quite well on an episode of Jeremy Kyle.

The final job that will stick with me is the time I attended a report of a lady finding her husband unconscious and not breathing after she had nipped to make them both their morning brew in bed. This guy was in his seventies and a large six foot strong-built man, with no medical conditions that they knew about. I attended quite quickly, as I was driving past their road when the job came in. On my arrival, I ran upstairs to find the male lay on his bed, covered up to his chest and not breathing. As much as I tried, I didn't have the strength to pull him off the bed, so decided that I had to start CPR where he was situated. I knew that the bed wouldn't offer enough resistance to allow the CPR to be successful, but this lady was looking at, me expecting me to help and I couldn't just do nothing. I got onto the bed and removed the covers to locate the correct area on the man's chest. It transpired that he slept naked. With every chest compression I did, his penis flapped from side to side. I was so embarrassed but just wanted the lady to see that I was doing something to help her husband. With every compression, it went from left to right, right to left and was extremely off-putting. I was so grateful when two big, burly paramedics arrived and helped me pull the man off the bed, onto the floor. When they placed the ECG on his chest, I had managed to keep his heart pumping until they got there, so they continued CPR all the way to the hospital where he sadly died.

The next day, I felt so sad for the lady that I took her a big bunch of flowers to offer my condolences; they were taken and the door shut in my face, I'm assuming because I hadn't managed to save him. But that's the police, you are only human.

FINAL THOUGHT

Whilst being a police officer for the past ten years, I have had my highs and lows. I absolutely loved my job because it enabled me to help people. I worked my way up to getting paid a large amount of money, which I once believed I could never do in anything else, due to my childhood and lack of education or academic grades. I was satisfied that I was working alongside graduates, yet being paid the same wage and doing the job better, due to my life experience. The only time I didn't enjoy my job was when politics got in the way. When I was told to arrest a female with severe learning difficulties for assaulting a care staff member, despite this being morally wrong in my opinion. When I was told to go and tell a rape victim that the case against her predator was being dropped because of lack of evidence. When I was told social services had given back young children to homes where I had removed them from due to the floor being littered with hypodermic needles and the parents being high as a kite on heroin. Politics of being micromanaged by supervisors that were trying to evidence a catalogue of examples to progress further up the ranking structure.

I loved seeing the smile on the face of every person that I helped. Treating people with respect and dignity. Being satisfied that I had done a good job and when I had not been satisfied, that I had learned from it. When I arrested many people, they generally thanked me before I retired from my shift for treating them with respect and not judging them. I was thanked on many occasions for never looking down on anyone, despite their circumstance. For going the extra mile to help. For sitting with a mental health patient for hours, rather than ignoring them. Talking to them, making them realise that they can and will get better. I've been thanked by families of people who had died, when I attended to pass the bad news, for not being a robot and crying with them, sharing their emotion. Thanked for believing in young people, when everyone else had washed their hands of them. It's easy to get bogged down as a cop and treat the regular missing people as a pain in the arse, forgetting that many of them are products of their upbringings. But spending that little bit of extra time without judgement allowed many of them to feel safe around me and allowed them to open up about their abuse, criminal history or poor home life. I am truly thankful for the past ten years of my life. I have helped many people and placed many offenders in prison. I do not regret one single incident or occasion as it has all shaped me into the person I am today.

When Andrew Summerscales died, I made the decision to leave the police. There were only so many people I could handle losing in such a cruel and emotive manner. I have done my time dealing with the negative side of life and feel like, due to the job, I developed a tainted view on society and the world as a whole. When I left, I explained to my supervision that I wanted to pretend that the world was a beautiful place for a while. I wanted to guarantee that each evening, I would return to cuddle my children and each morning I'd wake, and let them know how much I loved them.

This is by no means the end of my role in helping people. Over the past three years, I have trained at Lowe Martial Arts. I have become a black belt in full-contact kickboxing and throughout that time, I have also completed my Level one teaching qualification under the Cobra Martial Arts Association. I am lucky enough to work alongside my coach and best friend, Chris Lowe. I now strive to mentor young adults who have struggled in life. Many have struggled with their own personal battles, ranging from social anxieties to barriers to learning. My job now allows me to show these young people that they all have a bright future, no matter what their history. I assist them in gaining control of their lives, increasing self-confidence, self-belief and life skills. Alongside their martial arts courses, I assist them in academic learning of maths and English and applying for jobs or colleges when they become old enough. My job these days is the most rewarding job I have ever had. I will make sure these people I work with know that I will never give up on them and will always be there to help them, should they require it.

The job also allows me to follow my passion of fighting competitively in full-contact kickboxing. In 2015/2016 I have achieved and defended two full-contact amateur Kickboxing British titles. One for Golden Belt and one for CMAA. I recently fought one of the best females in the country in Liverpool, for a European title Eliminator and won. Next year, 2017, will be my greatest yet.

The future is bright x